MW00899536

Engage Students with UDL

A Practical Guide to Universal Design for Learning with Guideline, Strategies and Lesson Plans for Teachers

ROBERTO RUSSO

Engage Students with UDL: A Practical Guide to Universal Design for Learning with Guideline, Strategies and Lesson Plans for Teachers
© Copyright (2024) All rights reserved.
Written by Roberto Russo

Additional Resources for UDL Implementation

Dear Fellow Educators,

During the research and writing process of this book, I accumulated a considerable amount of material that, due to space constraints and coherence, couldn't be included in the pages you hold.

However, these additional resources can be of great practical value.

I have prepared a supplementary **Practical Guide** that includes a curated collection of thematic web resources selected for their relevance and applicability;

These resources are available free of charge to complement the book you've purchased. To access them, you can either:

Visit the web address: https://teachfizz.com/udltools

Or **Scan the QR code** below:

If you find these resources useful, I would appreciate you sharing a brief feedback or reflection on your experience. Your comments and suggestions are valuable to me and motivate me to continue developing material that can truly support your daily work.

With appreciation and gratitude,

Roberto Russo

Table of Contents

Introduction

In every classroom, educators face the challenge of engaging a diverse group of students. Picture a typical scene: some students are fully immersed, raising their hands, and contributing to discussions, while others appear disengaged, doodling, daydreaming, or, worse, causing distractions. This disparity is a reality in today's educational landscape, where classrooms are more diverse than ever, encompassing students with varying backgrounds, learning styles, abilities, and interests. The goal for educators is clear: to engage all students and ensure that every learner feels included and motivated. But how can this be achieved effectively? The answer lies in the principles of UDL).

This book is designed to equip educators with the knowledge and tools needed to create inclusive and engaging learning environments. UDL is an educational framework that recognizes the diversity of learners and provides flexible approaches to teaching and assessment. This book offers a clear, actionable guide to implementing UDL in the classroom, with practical strategies, tools, and lesson plans. It aims to bridge the gap between theory and practice, showing how UDL principles can be seamlessly integrated into everyday teaching.

Modern classrooms are defined by their diversity. Each student comes with a unique set of strengths, challenges, and learning preferences, making it essential for educators to move beyond one-size-fits-all teaching methods. UDL provides a robust framework for this by advocating for flexible teaching practices that accommodate all learners, recognizing that there is no "average" student. Instead, UDL encourages teachers to proactively design their lessons to support multiple means of engagement, representation, action and expression, ensuring that every student has equal access to learning opportunities.

Implementing UDL is more than just acknowledging the diversity of learners; it is about fostering an inclusive environment where all students can achieve their fullest potential. UDL does not mean lowering expectations but rather providing multiple pathways for students to meet high standards. This approach is akin to designing an accessible building: just as ramps, wide doorways, and elevators ensure access for everyone, UDL practices ensure all students can engage with and benefit from the curriculum. By anticipating and planning for learner variability, educators can transform their classrooms into inclusive, dynamic spaces that cater to a wide range of learning needs.

Given the evolving landscape of education, now is the ideal time to adopt UDL strategies. The push towards greater inclusivity and improved learning outcomes requires innovative approaches that accommodate diverse learner profiles. The strategies outlined in this book are not meant to add to your workload; rather, they are designed to make teaching and learning more effective and enjoyable for both educators and students. The implementation of UDL principles can significantly enhance student engagement and achievement, transforming the educational experience for all involved.

The book is structured to build your understanding and confidence in applying UDL. It begins with an exploration of the foundational principles, offering a solid theoretical grounding. From there, it moves to practical applications, including optimizing classroom environments and developing innovative instructional and assessment strategies aligned with UDL. Each chapter is packed with detailed guidance, tips, and tools to help educators apply UDL principles in their daily teaching practices effectively.

In addition to theoretical insights, the book provides real-world examples and case studies from educators who have successfully integrated UDL into their classrooms. These stories illustrate the transformative power of UDL and offer practical advice on overcoming common challenges. To further support educators, the book includes reflective exercises and practical questions designed to help you assess your current practices and identify growth opportunities.

By the end of this book, you will not only understand UDL principles but also feel equipped to integrate them into your teaching with ease. You will be empowered to create a more inclusive, engaging, and effective learning environment for all your students. Remember, UDL is not about adding more to your teaching load; it is about using a framework that makes teaching and learning more efficient and rewarding for everyone.

Chapter 1

Introduction to Universal Design for Learning

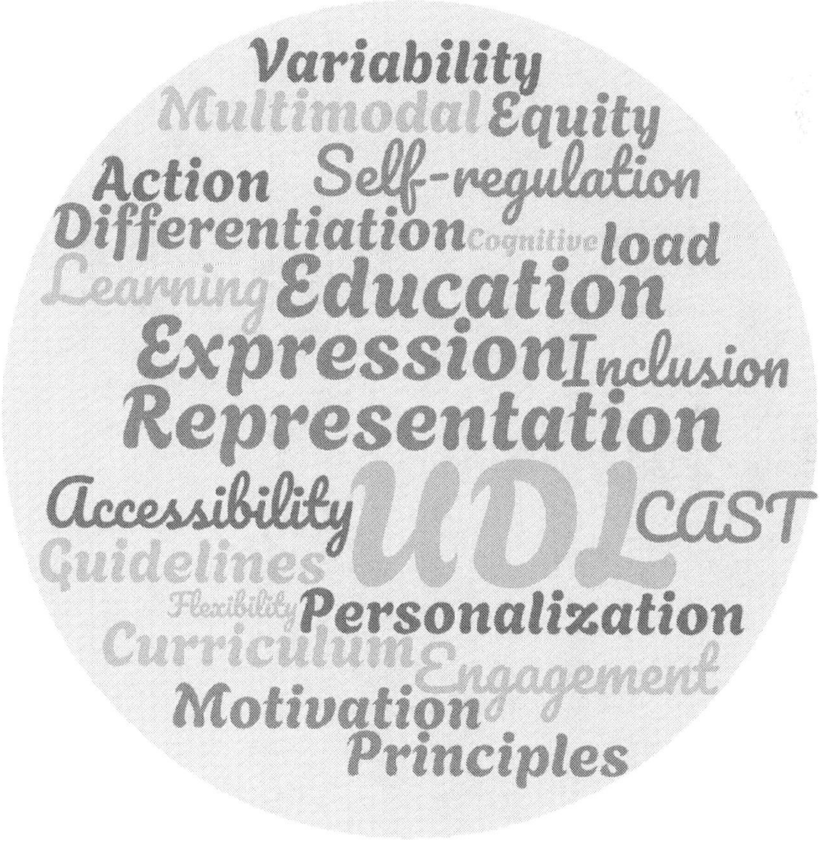

Universal Design for Learning (UDL) is a teaching **framework** that aims to create flexible and inclusive educational environments, addressing the diverse needs of all learners. The essence of UDL lies in its commitment to removing barriers to learning, ensuring that each student has the opportunity to engage with the curriculum in meaningful and effective ways. Understanding the origins and evolution of UDL provides a comprehensive insight into its foundational principles and highlights its significance in contemporary education.

This chapter explores the **historical development of UDL**, tracing its origins from initial special education initiatives to its current status as a comprehensive approach endorsed by educational systems globally. We will examine the core principles of UDL— **Engagement, Representation, and Action & Expression**—and discuss how these principles promote inclusive learning environments. Additionally, we will examine the impact of important legislation, such as the **Individuals with Disabilities Education Act (IDEA)** and the **Americans with Disabilities Act (ADA)**, in advocating for the implementation of UDL practices. Finally, the chapter will address the international momentum for UDL, showcasing how regions like Europe, Australia, and Canada have advanced inclusive education practices.

Origins and Evolution of UDL

The term "Universal Design" was coined by architect **Ronald L. Mace** in 1985. He defined it as the design of products and environments that are inherently accessible to all people without requiring adaptations or specialized solutions. This foundational idea expanded into the field of education through the pioneering efforts of **CAST (Center for Applied Special Technology)**, an American research group. CAST sought to enhance existing curricula by making them more accessible and adaptable to the individual variability of students, utilizing flexible goals, inclusive methods, materials, and assessment processes.

The **UDL Guidelines** (udlguidelines.cast.org), most recently revised in 2024 (version 3.0), articulate three fundamental principles supported by neuroscientific research, which are essential for ensuring that all students have access to effective learning opportunities:

1. **Multiple Means of Engagement:** Providing diverse ways to stimulate interest and motivation for learning.
2. **Multiple Means of Representation:** Offering various methods to present information and content.
3. **Multiple Means of Action and Expression:** Allowing students to demonstrate their knowledge in different ways.

As educational paradigms evolved, so too did the legislative landscape, which increasingly recognized the value of inclusive practices. **IDEA**, first enacted in 1975, was a landmark law mandating that students with disabilities receive a free and appropriate public education tailored to their unique needs. This legislation underscored the importance of accommodating diverse learners within general education settings, paving the way for the UDL movement. Similarly, the **ADA**, enacted in 1990, further emphasized the elimination of discrimination and the assurance of accessibility in all areas of public life, including education. These

13

legislative frameworks were instrumental in promoting UDL principles, urging schools to develop more inclusive educational practices.

As these legislative mandates were implemented, educators recognized that the benefits of UDL extended beyond students with disabilities, enhancing learning outcomes for all students. In recent years, educational shifts, driven by technological advancements and a greater emphasis on **inclusive classroom cultures**, have further accelerated the adoption of UDL principles. Digital tools and resources now offer educators unprecedented opportunities to design dynamic, adaptable learning experiences. Interactive multimedia, for example, caters to diverse learning preferences, while assistive technologies provide personalized support tailored to specific student needs.

Global Implementation and Impact of UDL

UDL's adoption has transcended national boundaries, becoming a global movement toward more **equitable and inclusive education**. In Europe, initiatives by the **European Agency for Special Needs and Inclusive Education** have actively promoted UDL principles through various projects, helping member states develop policies that align with UDL. In Australia, the **National Disability Insurance Scheme (NDIS)** highlights the importance of accessible and inclusive education, with schools increasingly adopting UDL practices to cater to the diverse needs of their students. Similarly, in Canada, the **UDL Implementation and Research Network (UDL-IRN)** has been pivotal in advancing UDL practices, offering professional development, resource sharing, and research opportunities to enhance the adoption of UDL in Canadian schools.

These examples illustrate the widespread acceptance and implementation of UDL globally. Countries are increasingly incorporating UDL principles into their educational frameworks, reflecting a collective commitment to ensuring that all students, regardless of ability or background, have access to high-quality education.

Key Principles: Engagement, Representation, Action & Expression

Understanding the Core Principles of UDL

UDL provides a framework for optimizing teaching and learning by recognizing the variability in how humans learn. The three fundamental principles - **Engagement, Representation, and Action & Expression** - provide a framework for developing instructional objectives, methods, materials, and evaluations that cater to a wide range of learners.

Engagement: Fostering Active Participation

Recent advances in **psychology and neurobiology** underscore the integration of cognitive processes with motivational and emotional systems, influencing learning outcomes. Effective engagement involves creating a classroom environment that fosters **self-esteem, a sense of self-efficacy**, and a cooperative atmosphere rather than a competitive one. This environment should be rich in **feedback, encouragement, and clear guidance**, which supports students' learning processes and enhances their motivation to engage.

A classroom climate that supports emotional well-being and self-regulation is vital. Engaging students involves aligning instructional strategies with their interests and providing opportunities for **active, hands-on learning**, such as through group discussions, collaborative projects, and peer-assisted learning activities. This approach not only helps students acquire knowledge but also develops **metacognitive skills** and a positive attitude towards learning.

Representation: Diversifying the Ways Information is Presented

Students learn in different ways. Some students do well with pictures, while others like to hear information or touch things. The UDL principle of **multiple means of representation** suggests that information should be presented in different ways to meet the needs of all students. This includes modifying traditional materials—such as using legible fonts and ample spacing for printed texts—and incorporating multimedia elements like videos, animations, and interactive graphics. Such strategies help reduce cognitive overload and support deeper comprehension.

Using **visual organizers** like graphs, charts, and concept maps can also enhance understanding by providing clear visual representations of information. These tools help students systematically organize knowledge, making it easier to grasp complex concepts and retain information.

Action & Expression: Offering Multiple Ways to Demonstrate Knowledge

UDL emphasizes the need to provide students with **multiple avenues to express their learning**. Recognizing that students differ in how they best demonstrate their knowledge—whether through writing, speaking, or creative projects—allows for more personalized and effective assessment. Flexible assessment options, such as **oral presentations, written essays, digital portfolios, and concept maps**, empower students to choose the method that aligns with their strengths and provides a more accurate representation of their understanding.

By leveraging a variety of assessment tools, educators can gain a more comprehensive understanding of student learning and provide more targeted feedback that supports growth and development.

Interconnectedness of Principles: A Synergistic Approach

The true strength of UDL lies in the **interconnectedness of its principles**. When combined, Engagement, Representation, and Action & Expression create an inclusive educational environment where all students have the opportunity to succeed. The synergy among these principles ensures that students are not only motivated to learn but also have access to the content in ways that make sense to them and can demonstrate their knowledge in ways that are most effective for them.

By embracing the UDL framework, educators can foster a more dynamic, inclusive, and equitable classroom that accommodates the needs of all learners, ultimately enhancing educational outcomes and creating a more engaging and supportive learning environment.

UDL Guidelines

Design Multiple Means of Engagement	Design Multiple Means of Representation	Design Multiple Means of Action & Expression
Guideline 7 **Design Options for Welcoming Interests & Identities** 7.1 Optimize choice and autonomy 7.2 Optimize relevance, value, and authenticity 7.3 Nurture joy and play 7.4 Address biases, threats, and distractions	**Guideline 1** **Design Options for Perception** 1.1 Support opportunities to customize the display of information 1.2 Support multiple ways to perceive information 1.3 Represent a diversity of perspectives and identities in authentic ways	**Guideline 4** **Design Options for Interaction** 4.1 Vary and honor the methods for response, navigation, and movement 4.2 Optimize access to accessible materials and assistive and accessible technologies and tools
Guideline 8 **Design Options for Sustaining Effort & Persistence** 8.1 Clarify the meaning and purpose of goals 8.2 Optimize challenge and support 8.3 Foster collaboration, interdependence, and collective learning 8.4 Foster belonging and community 8.5 Offer action-oriented feedback	**Guideline 2** **Design Options for Language & Symbols** 2.1 Clarify vocabulary, symbols, and language structures 2.2 Support decoding of text, mathematical notation, and symbols 2.3 Cultivate understanding and respect across languages and dialects 2.4 Address biases in the use of language and symbols 2.5 Illustrate through multiple media	**Guideline 5** **Design Options for Expression & Communication** 5.1 Use multiple media for communication 5.2 Use multiple tools for construction, composition, and creativity 5.3 Build fluencies with graduated support for practice and performance 5.4 Address biases related to modes of expression and communication
Guideline 9 **Design Options for Emotional Capacity** 9.1 Recognize expectations, beliefs, and motivations 9.2 Develop awareness of self and others 9.3 Promote individual and collective reflection 9.4 Cultivate empathy and restorative practices	**Guideline 3** **Design Options for Building Knowledge** 3.1 Connect prior knowledge to new learning 3.2 Highlight and explore patterns, critical features, big ideas, and relationships 3.3Cultivate multiple ways of knowing and making meaning 3.4 Maximize transfer and generalization	**Guideline 6** **Design Options for Strategy Development** 6.1 Set meaningful goals 6.2 Anticipate and plan for challenges 6.3 Organize information and resources 6.4 Enhance capacity for monitoring progress 6.5 Challenge exclusionary practices

Reference: https://udlguidelines.cast.org/

References

CAST (2024). Universal Design for Learning Guidelines version 3.0.
https://udlguidelines.cast.org/
Individuals with Disabilities Education Act (IDEA)
https://sites.ed.gov/idea/
Americans with Disabilities Act (ADA) https://www.ada.gov/
European Agency for Special Needs and Inclusive Education
https://www.european-agency.org/
National Disability Insurance Scheme (NDIS) https://www.ndis.gov.au/
Universal Design for Learning Implementation and Research Network (UDL-IRN) https://udl-irn.org/

Chapter 2

Preparing Your Classroom Space for UDL

As discussed earlier, the term "Universal Design" initially emerged from architecture, aiming to create spaces with maximum flexibility and accessibility for all users. Applying this concept to the educational setting requires designing a classroom environment that supports the diverse needs of learners by implementing UDL principles. A well-prepared classroom can significantly enhance learning by making the environment more responsive to the variability of all students.

Flexible seating arrangements are a critical aspect of creating an inclusive classroom environment. The flexible seating arrangements allow students to choose the best seating option for their learning preferences and needs, promoting a sense of autonomy and comfort. Choices such as bean bags, standing desks, and floor cushions provide students with a variety of options, creating a more inclusive and adaptable learning space. Moreover, establishing clear guidelines for the use and care of these seating options helps maintain their effectiveness as tools for enhancing student engagement and comfort.

Additionally, the **strategic use of bulletin boards** plays a significant role in providing visual support and enhancing learning within the classroom. These boards can serve as dynamic displays for essential information, learning objectives, and interactive content tailored to diverse learners. For instance, visual learners benefit from prominently displayed charts and graphics, while interactive elements encourage active student participation and critical thinking. By creating distinct zones within the classroom for various activities and incorporating personalized learning stations, teachers can cater more effectively to the unique needs and preferences of each student.

Create Flexible Spaces

To equip teachers with strategies for arranging seating that accommodates various learning styles and fosters inclusivity, it is essential to understand the importance of flexible seating options. Providing various seating choices like bean bags, floor cushions, or standing desks can significantly impact student comfort and autonomy.

Flexible seating options allow students to choose what works best for them on any given day, fostering an environment where they feel physically comfortable and mentally prepared to engage in learning activities. For instance, a student who has difficulty focusing while seated at a traditional desk may find that a standing desk helps them stay more engaged. Similarly, bean bags or floor cushions offer a more relaxed seating arrangement that might benefit students who need a break from conventional seating.

When implementing flexible seating, it's important to establish guidelines to ensure effective use and maintenance. Teachers should explain the purpose of different seating options and set clear expectations for their use.

Encourage students to try out various seats during different activities to find what best supports their learning style. Regularly rotating seating assignments can also help prevent students from becoming too reliant on one particular type of seat, ensuring they remain adaptable and open to change. Additionally, setting rules for the care and upkeep of seating areas will help maintain a clean and organized classroom environment.

Zoning the classroom is another essential strategy for creating a supportive learning environment. By dividing the classroom into distinct areas for different activities, teachers can help students navigate the space more effectively and choose environments that suit their current tasks. For example, a quiet area designated for independent work can be separated from a space intended for collaborative group projects. This supports different learning tasks and helps make transitions between activities smoother. Clear signage and visual cues can aid in delineating these zones, helping students quickly identify where they should be and what behavior is expected in each area.

Incorporating **movement-friendly layouts** within the classroom is crucial to accommodating diverse learning needs and promoting a dynamic learning atmosphere. Ensuring pathways are clear and unobstructed allows for fluid movement throughout the space, reducing the chances of distraction or disruption. This layout increases opportunities for physical engagement, which can stimulate thought processes and enhance collaboration among students. A study by the American Journal of Public Health found that incorporating movement breaks and allowing students to move around improved attention and cognitive performance. Therefore, promoting movement in the layout can profoundly impact student engagement and learning outcomes.

Teachers should consider arranging desks and tables in ways that facilitate both individual and group work. For example, having some desks in rows and others clustered together allows students to switch between solo tasks and group collaboration easily. Providing ample space for students to walk around without disturbing their classmates can encourage participation and reduce feelings of confinement, making the classroom a more inviting place.

Personalized learning stations further enhance the UDL principles by addressing the unique needs and preferences of each student. These stations can be tailored to various learning styles, offering different activities and resources that cater to auditory, visual, kinesthetic, and other learning modalities. For example, a learning station dedicated to visual learners might include graphic organizers, charts, and posters, while a station for kinesthetic learners could feature hands-on materials like manipulatives and tactile resources. Empowering students to choose how they engage with content through personalized learning stations promotes ownership of their learning journey and encourages self-directed exploration.

To implement personalized learning stations effectively, teachers should observe and understand their students' preferences and strengths. Gathering feedback from students about which activities and materials they find most engaging can provide valuable insights for setting up these stations. Rotating the materials and activities periodically keeps the stations fresh and interesting, encouraging continuous engagement and preventing boredom. Incorporating technology, such as tablets or computers with educational software, can further enrich these learning stations and provide interactive experiences that cater to different learning styles.

Engaging students in the design of their learning environment can also cultivate a sense of ownership and accountability. By involving students in imagining and creating their ideal learning spaces, teachers can cultivate a more inclusive and motivating environment. Online platforms like **Classroom Architect, Kaplan Floor Planner, KI Classroom Planner, and SmartDraw** provide interactive tools for designing and customizing classroom spaces, turning space design into a collaborative and engaging activity.

Classroom Design Tools

Classroom Architect:
https://www.quorumlearning.com/classroom-architect/
Kaplan Floor Planner:
https://www.kaplanco.com/resources/floorPlanner.asp
KI Classroom Planner: https://www.ki.com/design-resources/classroom-planner/
SmartDraw: https://www.smartdraw.com/

Effective Use of Bulletin Boards for Visual Support

Bulletin boards are invaluable tools for creating a visually engaging and supportive learning environment. UDL emphasizes the need for multiple ways for students to access, engage with, and demonstrate their understanding of content. Bulletin boards are effective in providing visual support for diverse learners.

One effective strategy for utilizing bulletin boards is **strategic information display**. By prominently displaying key information and learning objectives, teachers can reinforce learning and aid memory retention. Visual learners, in particular, benefit from having critical information accessible and easy to reference. Learning objectives, key concepts, vocabulary, and important dates can all be prominently displayed. For instance, a math class might feature a bulletin board with essential questions, formulas, and problem-solving steps for the current unit. This approach not only helps students retain vital information but also reduces cognitive overload by providing a clear and organized reference point.

Interactive bulletin boards further enhance engagement by actively involving students in the learning process. These boards can be designed to cultivate a sense of community, enhance critical thinking skills, and stimulate student engagement. For example, a literature class might have a bulletin board featuring a "question of the week" where students can post their responses or interpretations using sticky notes. Alternatively, a science class might use a bulletin board to facilitate a running inquiry on a current experiment, where students contribute hypotheses or observations. Such interactive elements transform bulletin boards into dynamic learning spaces that foster active engagement with the content and peer interaction.

Cultural and thematic representation on bulletin boards promotes a sense of belonging among students by reflecting diverse cultures and relatable themes. Displaying content that highlights cultural celebrations, historical figures from various backgrounds, or thematic projects that connect curriculum topics to real-world issues can enrich students' understanding and appreciation of diversity. For example, a social studies classroom might showcase a timeline of significant historical events from different cultures, highlighting contributions from diverse groups. This practice not only enhances students' knowledge but also prepares them for a multicultural society by fostering respect and appreciation for diversity.

Maintaining **relevance and interest** in bulletin boards involves regularly updating the content to reflect current topics and student work. For instance, after completing a unit on ecosystems, a science class might update its bulletin board to feature student projects, diagrams, and recent findings on environmental conservation. This approach not only showcases student achievements but also encourages reflection on learning progress. By rotating content regularly, bulletin boards remain vibrant and integral to the classroom environment.

To maximize the effectiveness of bulletin boards, **guidelines** for their use should be established. For information display, it is important to organize the board into sections dedicated to specific types of information, such as learning objectives, vocabulary, and key dates. Clear, well-defined headings and color differentiation can assist students in quickly finding necessary information. Additionally, the use of visuals such as charts, graphs, and images can further improve understanding and memory retention.

For **interactive bulletin boards**, guidelines include providing structured opportunities for student engagement, such as designating time for contributions or incorporating board interaction into class activities. It is also beneficial to establish rules for respectful and constructive participation, particularly when students share personal opinions or creative ideas.

Dynamic updates require a systematic approach. Setting a regular schedule for updating bulletin boards—whether weekly or at the end of each unit—helps keep content fresh and engaging. Involving students in the process of updating the boards can also be a valuable learning experience. Assigning roles or creating a rotation system for student contributions not only distributes the workload but also fosters a sense of ownership and pride in their classroom environment.

By thoughtfully preparing the classroom environment through UDL principles, teachers can create a more inclusive, engaging, and effective learning space that accommodates the diverse needs of all students.

Digital Platforms for Virtual Bulletin Boards

Padlet (https://padlet.com/)
A versatile platform that allows for the creation of interactive virtual bulletin boards. It can effectively replicate the concept of a physical bulletin board in a digital environment.

Seesaw (https://web.seesaw.me/)
A digital portfolio and learning platform that includes features for creating virtual bulletin boards where students can share their work and engage with peers.

Google Jamboard (https://edu.google.com/products/jamboard/)
A collaborative digital whiteboard that can be utilized to create interactive bulletin boards, fostering real-time collaboration among students and teachers.

Miro (https://miro.com/education-whiteboard/)
An online whiteboard platform offering templates for virtual bulletin boards and real-time collaboration, suitable for both synchronous and asynchronous learning environments.

Chapter 3

Managing the Inclusive Classroom

Implementing effective classroom management techniques is essential for creating an inclusive learning environment where every student feels valued and supported. The diversity in today's classrooms requires educators to adopt strategies that accommodate the varied needs, strengths, and learning styles of all students. An inclusive classroom environment not only prioritizes the academic development of students but also their social and emotional growth. Effective classroom management goes beyond enforcing rules; it encompasses creating a structured yet flexible setting that adapts to different learning styles, maximizes engagement, and minimizes disruptions.

This chapter delves into practical strategies to create a classroom atmosphere conducive to learning for all students. By addressing the unique challenges faced by each learner and ensuring smooth and predictable transitions between activities, educators can reduce disruptions and optimize learning opportunities. Techniques such as using visual timers, establishing structured transition areas, conducting pre-transition check-ins, and adopting flexible scheduling will be discussed in detail. These strategies are designed to reduce student confusion, anxiety, and stress, allowing them to focus and participate more effectively in their learning activities. Through this chapter, educators will learn how to implement these tools step-by-step and customize them to suit their specific classroom dynamics.

Creating Smoother Schedules and Transition Areas

Managing daily schedules and transitions effectively is crucial in an inclusive classroom setting. It ensures a supportive environment in which all students can thrive, regardless of their individual needs. Several strategies can facilitate smoother transitions and maintain a structured flow of activities.

Visual timers are powerful tools for managing classroom time and transitions. They help students understand time constraints and prepare for upcoming transitions, thereby reducing anxiety and enhancing focus. For example, projecting a countdown timer on the classroom wall provides a constant visual cue, helping students anticipate changes and adjust accordingly. This reduces the likelihood of distractions and keeps students engaged. Various types of visual timers, such as sand timers, digital countdowns, or app-based timers, can cater to different preferences and age groups. By incorporating these tools, educators can create a predictable and less stressful environment, particularly for students who struggle with changes in routine.

Structured transition areas also play a significant role in facilitating smooth transitions. By designating specific zones for different activities, such as reading corners, science tables, or art stations, educators can help students navigate the classroom more effectively and reduce confusion. Clear signage or color-coded zones can guide students to the appropriate areas, making transitions more seamless. Physical markers like rugs, tape, or movable dividers can further define these spaces and signal transitions effectively. Structured transition areas not only help students with organizational challenges but also promote independence and self-regulation.

Pre-transition check-ins are another effective strategy to prepare students for changes in activities. These check-ins can involve brief discussions, reminders, or collaborative planning sessions where students express their thoughts and preferences about upcoming transitions. Encouraging students to provide input helps them feel a sense of ownership and increases their engagement. For instance, before transitioning from a math lesson to a group activity, the teacher might ask students how they feel about the upcoming change and what could make the transition smoother. This proactive approach helps address potential anxieties and creates a more inclusive classroom environment.

Flexible scheduling is key to accommodating the diverse needs of learners. A rigid timetable may only suit some students, particularly those with varying attention spans or specific learning preferences. Offering choices in the daily schedule allows students to choose activities that align with their strengths and interests, creating a more personalized learning experience. For example, allowing students to choose between beginning the day with independent reading or a hands-on science experiment can enhance engagement by catering to their interests. This approach recognizes and respects the individuality of each student, fostering a more inclusive and adaptable classroom environment.

Establishing Effective Classroom Meetings

Regular classroom meetings are an essential strategy for building an inclusive learning environment. These meetings foster communication, create a sense of community, and help all students feel included and valued. When students feel heard and respected, their engagement and commitment to learning increases.

Collaborative goal-setting is a productive way to start these meetings. By involving students in setting both individual and collective goals, teachers can align diverse learners toward common objectives. For example, discussing and deciding on goals, such as maintaining a tidy classroom or supporting each other during group activities, fosters a sense of shared responsibility and pride. Using a structured framework, like **SMART goals (Specific, Measurable, Achievable, Relevant, Time-bound)**, ensures that all students can participate meaningfully in the goal-setting process, regardless of their individual needs.

S	**Specific**	Make your goal specific and narrow for more effective planning
M	**Misurable**	Make sure your goal and progress are misurable
A	**Achievable**	Make sure you can reasonably accomplish your goal within a certain time frame
R	**Relevant**	Your goal should allign with your values and long-term objectives
T	**Time-based**	Set a realistic but ambitious end date to clarify task priorization and increase motivation

Conflict resolution strategies are another crucial component of classroom meetings. Teaching students to handle disagreements constructively is vital for maintaining a supportive classroom community. Role-playing exercises are an effective method for practicing conflict resolution skills. By simulating scenarios where conflicts might arise, students can learn to navigate disagreements with empathy and effective communication. Establishing clear, simple rules for conflict resolution—such as "Listen to understand, not to argue" or "Seek a compromise that respects everyone's needs"—provides a framework for students to follow when conflicts occur.

Celebrating achievements regularly during classroom meetings can also enhance motivation and build a positive classroom culture. Recognizing both individual and group accomplishments nurtures pride and encourages sustained effort and engagement. These celebrations need not be elaborate; even simple acknowledgments like verbal praise or showcasing student work can significantly boost morale. Dedicating time to highlight positive contributions—whether academic or behavioral—helps cultivate an atmosphere of appreciation and recognition, motivating students to strive for excellence.

Feedback mechanisms are equally vital for fostering an inclusive classroom environment. Establishing methods for both peer and teacher feedback encourages a culture of constructive communication and respect for diverse perspectives. Well-structured feedback systems, such as anonymous suggestion boxes, regular one-on-one check-ins, or guided peer review sessions, provide opportunities for students to express their thoughts and feelings. For example, after a group project, students could evaluate each other's contributions using structured prompts that focus on constructive feedback. This not only builds trust among peers but also teaches students the importance of receiving and giving feedback respectfully.

Incorporating these strategies into regular classroom meetings requires consistent effort and planning. Educators should strive to create a secure and inclusive environment where every student feels free to express their thoughts and experiences. Techniques like **"think-pair-share"** can help quieter students feel more confident about voicing their thoughts. In this method, students first reflect individually, then discuss their ideas with a partner, and finally share with the larger group. This tiered approach reduces the stress of speaking in front of the whole class and promotes wider participation.

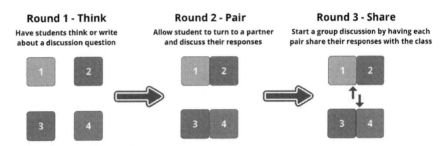

Round 1 - Think
Have students think or write about a discussion question

Round 2 - Pair
Allow student to turn to a partner and discuss their responses

Round 3 - Share
Start a group discussion by having each pair share their responses with the class

Think-Pair-Share Process

Using **visual aids and multimedia resources** in these meetings can further engage students and cater to different learning styles. Videos, infographics, and interactive whiteboards can make discussions more dynamic and accessible, particularly when explaining complex concepts or addressing diverse linguistic needs.

Establishing a routine for classroom meetings is also essential. Scheduling these meetings at consistent times, such as the beginning or end of the week, integrates them seamlessly into the classroom schedule and reinforces their importance. Regular meetings foster a customary practice of open communication and community building, which is crucial for an inclusive learning environment.

Involving students in meeting preparation and facilitation can enhance effectiveness. Assigning roles like facilitator, note-taker, or timekeeper helps students develop leadership skills and feel more invested in the classroom community. Rotating these roles ensures that all students have the opportunity to experience different aspects of meeting management, fostering a sense of responsibility and engagement.

By using these strategies, teachers can establish a more welcoming and encouraging classroom atmosphere, enabling all students to feel appreciated, esteemed, and driven to succeed.

Chapter 4

Leveraging Technology for UDL

Integrating **educational technology** is pivotal for enhancing the application of UDL in classrooms, promoting greater accessibility and engagement. Tools such as **blogs, videoconferencing, computational thinking platforms, gamification, and interactive e-books** provide diverse avenues for students to communicate, collaborate, and engage with content. These technologies enable new forms of **expression, problem-solving, and personalized learning**. When implemented strategically, these methods create dynamic and inclusive environments where every student can thrive.

This chapter examines how various digital tools can facilitate collaborative and engaging learning. Educators will explore how blogs enhance **reflective thinking** and **peer feedback**, how videoconferencing fosters global connections, and how computational thinking builds critical skills across disciplines. The role of gamification in boosting motivation and how interactive e-books provide **customizable**, multimodal learning experiences will also be covered. Moreover, this chapter discusses how these tools create inclusive environments, enhance digital literacy, and prepare students for future challenges. Through these strategies, educators can achieve a more equitable educational experience, equipping learners with essential skills for the digital age.

Using Blogs and Videoconferencing for Collaborative Learning

Enhancing communication through blogs

Effective communication is fundamental in diverse classrooms. Blogs serve as a dynamic platform for students to express ideas and engage in **reflective thinking**. Through regular blog posts, students articulate their understanding, pose questions, and reflect on their learning journey. This exercise not only deepens comprehension but also fosters a culture of inquiry. For instance, writing about historical events or scientific discoveries allows students to analyze and connect new knowledge with existing understanding critically.

Blogs also enable students to give **peer feedback**, allowing them to comment on each other's work. This interaction fosters a sense of community and collaborative learning. Students gain insights from diverse perspectives, enhancing their understanding and critical thinking skills. Engaging with peers' viewpoints broadens their intellectual horizons, promoting a more inclusive classroom atmosphere.

Guideline: Encourage consistent blogging and peer interaction to maintain a dynamic, collaborative learning environment.

Engaging students with videoconferencing

Videoconferencing tools, such as Zoom and Microsoft Teams, offer real-time engagement opportunities, bridging geographical divides. These platforms facilitate in-person interactions, creating a more engaging and lively learning environment. Through live discussions, students refine verbal communication skills and gain confidence in presenting ideas. This immediate feedback loop improves engagement and participation, which is vital for effective learning.

Furthermore, videoconferencing enables global connections, enriching the curriculum with diverse perspectives. Virtual guest lectures from international experts provide unique learning opportunities. For example, inviting a scientist to discuss climate change or a historian to talk about global events can make learning more relevant and engaging. Group projects conducted via video meetings also promote teamwork, which is essential for developing social skills and collaborative competencies.

Creating inclusive classroom environments

Blogs and videoconferencing contribute significantly to inclusivity by providing platforms for all students to express themselves. These tools are particularly advantageous for students who may feel hesitant to speak up in traditional settings. Blogs allow them to communicate their ideas in writing, while videoconferencing offers multiple participation options, such as chat functions and breakout rooms. These features ensure all students, including remote or mobility-impaired individuals, can fully engage in classroom activities.

> **Guideline**: Utilize varied participation features in videoconferencing to accommodate different comfort levels and ensure inclusive engagement.

Building digital literacy skills

Incorporating blogs and videoconferencing enhances **digital literacy**, a critical skill in today's educational landscape. Writing blogs teaches students online content creation, including formatting, editing, and publishing. They learn about digital citizenship, understanding online behavior norms, copyright laws, and proper citation practices. Videoconferencing tools, on the other hand, teach virtual communication etiquette and technical troubleshooting skills, preparing students for a digital future.

41

Incorporating E-Books and Interactive Content

E-books and **interactive content** have transformed traditional educational practices, providing more accessible and engaging learning opportunities. These resources cater to diverse learning needs through multiple formats—text, audio, and visual. For instance, audio versions support students with reading difficulties, while visual aids enhance understanding for visual learners.

Interactive elements like embedded quizzes provide immediate feedback, which is crucial for self-assessment and maintaining motivation. Videos and simulations provide dynamic explanations of complex concepts, making abstract ideas more tangible. This multimodal approach aligns with UDL principles, catering to varied learning preferences.

E-books also support **collaborative learning** through shared notes and annotations, promoting deeper understanding through peer interaction. Students can engage with different interpretations, fostering critical analysis and collaborative discussion. Additionally, analytics features track student progress, allowing teachers to provide targeted support and adjust instruction to meet individual needs.

Guideline: Regularly update and review e-Book content to ensure engagement and alignment with learning objectives.

Promoting Engagement through Gamification and Adaptive Learning Technologies

Gamification and adaptive learning technologies are effective strategies for increasing engagement and supporting individualized learning. Gamification incorporates game-like elements like points and badges to motivate students through rewards and challenges, making learning more interactive and enjoyable, especially for those who struggle with traditional methods.

Adaptive learning tech adjusts content based on student performance in real-time, ensuring personalized pacing and support for every student. Such technologies foster **self-paced** learning, which is crucial for diverse classrooms, as they accommodate varying learning speeds and styles.

Real-time feedback from these tools enables timely interventions, preventing minor issues from becoming significant obstacles. This proactive approach ensures continuous progress and engagement, aligning with UDL principles.

Guideline: Integrate gamification and adaptive learning technologies to cater to diverse learning needs and enhance engagement.

Foster Computational Thinking

Integrating coding and computational thinking activities into the curriculum develops critical skills while adhering to UDL principles. Platforms like **Code.org** and **Scratch** offer accessible and engaging coding lessons, teaching valuable technical skills and enhancing logical reasoning, creativity, and problem-solving abilities.

These platforms support multiple means of action and expression, allowing students to demonstrate understanding through creative projects rather than traditional assessments. Collaborative features also promote peer learning, fostering a supportive community of learners.

Guideline: Use coding platforms to introduce computational thinking and encourage collaborative projects to enhance problem solving skills.

Block programming example on Scratch

Technology Platforms

In today's educational landscape, a variety of innovative platforms facilitate knowledge sharing and provide formative feedback. These tools support continuous assessment and feedback, moving beyond traditional evaluation methods. By offering diverse channels for sharing work and ideas, they align with UDL principles, promoting an inclusive and dynamic learning environment.

These platforms empower students to participate actively in their learning journey, fostering self-reflection and peer assessment. As education evolves, these tools represent cutting-edge solutions that enhance the sharing of knowledge and the delivery of meaningful, formative feedback.

Blogs:

WordPress (https://wordpress.com/)
or Blogger (https://www.blogger.com/):
These popular blogging platforms offer user-friendly interfaces for creating and managing student blogs. They provide customizable templates and various multimedia integration options, allowing students to express their ideas creatively.

Kidblog (https://kidblog.org/):
A kid-friendly, education-focused blogging platform designed specifically for K-12 students. It offers a safe, controlled environment where teachers can monitor and approve posts before they go live, ensuring appropriate content and digital citizenship.

Flipgrid (https://info.flipgrid.com/):
While primarily a video discussion platform, Flipgrid can be used for video blogging. Students can record short video responses to prompts, fostering verbal communication skills and allowing for creative expression through visual means.

Videoconferencing

Zoom (https://zoom.us/)
or **Google Meet** (https://meet.google.com/):
These widely used videoconferencing tools offer features like screen sharing, breakout rooms, and chat functions. They're excellent for virtual classrooms, allowing for real-time interaction and collaboration.

Microsoft Teams
(https://www.microsoft.com/en-us/microsoft-teams/):
A comprehensive collaboration platform that integrates videoconferencing with file sharing, chat, and other productivity tools. It's particularly useful for long-term projects and ongoing class discussions.

Skype in the Classroom (https://education.skype.com/):
A free global community that connects classrooms worldwide. It facilitates virtual field trips, guest speaker sessions, and cultural exchange projects, broadening students' perspectives.

Organization and sharing

Google Classroom
(https://edu.google.com/products/classroom/):
A free web service that streamlines the process of sharing files between teachers and students. It integrates with other Google tools, making it easy to create and organize assignments, provide feedback, and communicate.

Padlet (https://padlet.com/):
A virtual bulletin board tool where students can post notes, images, links, and videos. It's great for brainstorming sessions, group projects, and showcasing work, allowing all students to contribute regardless of their comfort with verbal participation.

Nearpod (https://nearpod.com/):
An interactive lesson delivery platform that allows teachers to create engaging presentations with embedded quizzes, polls, and activities. It supports various learning styles and allows for both synchronous and asynchronous participation.

Mentimeter (https://www.mentimeter.com/):
A real-time polling and feedback tool that can be used during video lessons or in-person classes. It allows for anonymous responses, encouraging participation from students who might be hesitant to speak up.

Seesaw (https://web.seesaw.me/):
A digital portfolio platform where students can document their learning through photos, videos, drawings, and more. It facilitates parent engagement and allows for easy sharing of student work.

Wakelet (https://wakelet.com/): A content curation platform that allows teachers and students to collect and organize resources from across the web. It's great for research projects, creating digital storytelling, and sharing curated collections of learning materials.

EdPuzzle (https://edpuzzle.com/): A video editing tool that allows teachers to create interactive video lessons. Teachers can add questions, voice notes, and quizzes to existing videos, making passive video watching an active learning experience.

Design and literacy skills

Canva (https://www.canva.com/):
A graphic design platform that simplifies the creation of visually appealing blog posts, presentations, and infographics. It helps students develop visual communication skills and understand the principles of design.

Grammarly (https://www.grammarly.com/):
An AI-powered writing assistant that helps improve grammar, spelling, and style. It's useful for enhancing students' writing skills across all digital communication platforms.

Digital Citizenship curriculum by Common Sense Education (https://www.commonsense.org/education/digital-citizenship):
A comprehensive K-12 curriculum that covers topics like online safety, privacy, and ethical behavior. It helps students navigate the digital world responsibly and effectively.

E-book and interactive content

Epic! (https://www.getepic.com/):
A digital library with thousands of e-books, audiobooks, and videos for students up to age 12. It offers personalized recommendations based on reading level and interests.

Book Creator (https://bookcreator.com/):
An intuitive tool for students to create their interactive e-books. It supports text, images, audio, and video, allowing for multi-modal storytelling and content creation.

Actively Learn (https://www.activelylearn.com/):
A platform for embedding questions, notes, and discussions directly within digital texts. It promotes active reading and allows teachers to monitor comprehension in real-time.

Pear Deck (https://www.peardeck.com/):
An interactive presentation tool that integrates with Google Slides or PowerPoint. It allows teachers to embed formative assessments and engage every student in real-time during lessons.

Coding

Code.org (https://code.org).
Code.org offers free programming courses for students of all ages. It's particularly famous for its "Hour of Code" initiative, which introduces coding to millions of students worldwide.

Scratch (https://scratch.mit.edu)
Created by MIT, Scratch is a visual programming platform ideal for beginners and elementary to middle school students. It allows users to create interactive stories, games, and animations.

Gamification

Kahoot! (https://kahoot.com/)
or **Quizizz** (https://quizizz.com/):
Game-based learning platforms that turn quizzes into exciting competitions. They increase engagement through colorful interfaces, music, and friendly competition.

Panquiz (https://panquiz.com).
Panquiz is an easy-to-use online platform for creating subject-specific quizzes. With an intuitive interface and AI support, it helps educators quickly design customized quizzes for various subjects, offering suggestions and optimizing questions to enhance the learning experience.

Classscraft (https://www.classcraft.com/):
An immersive role-playing game that transforms the classroom experience. Students create avatars, earn points for positive behaviors, and work together on quests tied to the curriculum.

Duolingo (https://www.duolingo.com/):
A gamified language learning app that uses short, fun lessons to teach vocabulary and grammar. It adapts to the learner's pace and uses streaks and rewards to encourage consistent practice.

IXL (https://www.ixl.com/):
An adaptive learning platform for math, language arts, science, and social studies. It adjusts questions based on student performance, providing a personalized learning experience.

Prodigy Math Game (https://www.prodigygame.com/):
A fantasy-themed game world where math challenges are seamlessly integrated into adventures. It adapts to each student's level and aligns with curriculum standards.

Khan Academy (https://www.khanacademy.org/):
A free online learning platform offering courses in various subjects. It provides personalized learning paths, immediate feedback, and detailed progress tracking.

Chapter 5

Inclusive Teaching Strategies and UDL

Every student brings a unique perspective to the classroom, each with distinct strengths, challenges, and preferred ways of learning. Educators have the crucial task of nurturing this diversity by employing **inclusive teaching** strategies that cater to all learners. This approach aligns with the principles of UDL, fostering an environment where each student's needs are met and everyone feels valued.

Inclusive teaching strategies are designed to move beyond traditional, one-size-fits-all methods. They encompass a variety of techniques that adapt to different learning styles and preferences, recognizing the rich diversity of the classroom. From collaborative projects that leverage peer learning to technology-enhanced experiences that visualize complex concepts, these strategies offer multiple pathways for engagement and understanding.

Understanding Inclusive Teaching Strategies

Inclusive teaching strategies are not arbitrary; they are carefully chosen to align with the core principles of UDL:

Engagement: Strategies like collaborative learning and peer interaction foster a sense of belonging and motivation by tapping into students' social needs.

Representation: Techniques that present information in diverse formats—text, visuals, hands-on activities—align with the UDL principle of providing multiple means of representation.

Action and Expression: Allowing students to demonstrate learning in various ways, such as through writing, speaking, or creative projects, supports the principle of multiple means of action and expression.

The challenge in implementing these strategies lies in their flexibility and adaptability. It requires educators to be innovative and willing to experiment with different methods, always tailoring them to the specific context of their classroom and the unique needs of their students. However, the rewards of creating a more inclusive and responsive learning environment are immense, fostering better engagement, understanding, and retention among all students.

This table shows a range of inclusive teaching strategies, providing links to UDL principles. The aim is not to provide a checklist but rather **a range of possibilities**—a set of adaptable strategies that educators can mix and match to best suit their classroom dynamics.

LEARNING STRATEGIES	DESCRIPTION	UDL GUIDELINES
Cooperative Learning	Students work together in small groups to achieve shared learning goals	8.3 Foster collaboration, interdependence, and collective learning
Peer Tutoring	Students teach other students, reinforcing their own learning	2.3 Cultivate understanding and respect across languages and dialects
Project-Based Learning	Students gain knowledge and skills by working on an extended project	5.2 Use multiple tools for construction, composition, and creativity
Flipped Classroom	Content delivered outside class, class time used for practice and discussion	1.2 Support multiple ways to perceive information
Multi-Sensory Instruction	Teaching using visual, auditory, and kinesthetic-tactile pathways	1.2 Support multiple ways to perceive information
Inquiry-Based Learning	Students formulate questions and investigate to find answers	.2 Optimize relevance, value, and authenticity
Gamification	Applying game-design elements in non-game contexts	7.3 Nurture joy and play
Blended Learning	Combining online educational materials with traditional classroom methods	7.1 Optimize choice and autonomy 1.1 Support opportunities to customize the display of information
Scaffolding	Providing temporary support to help learners progress	5.3 Build fluencies with graduated support for practice and performance
Think-Pair-Share	Students think individually, discuss with a partner, then share with the class	8.3 Foster collaboration, interdependence, and collective learning
Jigsaw	Students are organized into groups to work on different parts of a topic	8.3 Foster collaboration, interdependence, and collective learning
Mind Mapping	Visual diagrams used to organize information	2.5 Illustrate through multiple media
Role-Playing	Students act out scenarios to	5.1 Use multiple media

	understand different perspectives	for communication
Visual Thinking	Facilitating discussions of visual images	2.5 Illustrate through multiple media
Socratic Seminar	A formal discussion based on a text where the leader asks open-ended questions	9.2 Develop awareness of self and others
Story-Based Learning	Using narratives to convey information and engage learners	7.2 Optimize relevance, value, and authenticity
Experiential Learning	Learning through reflection on doing	5.2 Use multiple tools for construction, composition, and creativity
Assistive Technology Integration	Using technology to increase, maintain, or improve functional capabilities	1.1 Support opportunities to customize the display of information 4.2 Optimize access to accessible materials and assistive and accessible technologies and tools
Learning Stations	Different areas in the classroom where students work on various tasks	7.1 Optimize choice and autonomy
Culturally Responsive Teaching	Teaching that uses cultural knowledge, prior experiences, and performance styles of diverse students	7.2 Optimize relevance, value, and authenticity
Problem-Based Learning (PBL)	Students learn about a subject through the experience of solving an open-ended problem	7.2 Optimize relevance, value, and authenticity
Concept Mapping	Graphical tool for organizing and representing knowledge	3.2 Highlight and explore patterns, critical features, big ideas, and relationships
Digital Storytelling	Using digital tools to tell stories	5.1 Use multiple media for communication
Collaborative Problem Solving	Students work together to solve complex problems	8.3 Foster collaboration, interdependence, and collective learning
Reflective Journaling	Students write about their experiences and reflect on their learning	6.4 Enhance capacity for monitoring progress
Reciprocal	Students and teachers switch	8.3 Foster collaboration,

Teaching	roles in teaching and learning	interdependence, and collective learning
Mindfulness	Incorporating mindfulness practices into the learning environment	9.2 Develop awareness of self and others
Mastery Learning	Students must achieve a level of mastery before moving on to new content	6.4 Enhance capacity for monitoring progress
Virtual Field Trips	Using technology to visit places virtually	2.5 Illustrate through multiple media
Augmented Reality	Overlaying digital information onto the real world for learning purposes	2.5 Illustrate through multiple media
Gallery Walk	Students explore multiple texts or images that are placed around the room	7.1 Optimize choice and autonomy
Debate	Using structured debates to explore complex issues	5.1 Use multiple media for communication 2.3 Cultivate understanding and respect across languages and dialects
Simulations and Role Play	Recreating real-world scenarios for learning purposes	7.2 Optimize relevance, value, and authenticity
Visible Thinking Routines	Structured thinking processes that make thinking visible and explicit	6.2 Anticipate and plan for challenges

Using Music and Drawing as Instructional Tools

Integrating **music and drawing** into teaching can significantly enhance engagement and understanding among diverse learners. These creative methods activate different sensory modalities, making learning more inclusive and enjoyable.

Music can transform abstract concepts into memorable content through rhythmic patterns and catchy songs.
For example, historical facts or scientific terms set to familiar tunes can be more engaging and easier to remember than rote memorization.
Songs can simplify complex concepts into smaller, more understandable segments, which helps with better comprehension and memory retention. Teachers can either create original songs related to the curriculum or utilize existing educational music resources, using rhythm and repetition to reinforce key concepts.

Drawing encourages students to visualize concepts, making abstract ideas more tangible. Drawing what they learn helps students engage in deeper cognitive processing.
For instance, in a biology class, drawing the stages of a cell division process can help students understand and retain the sequence of events more effectively. In a history lesson, illustrating key events or figures can aid in grasping the relationships and timelines, fostering a more comprehensive understanding of historical contexts.

Combining these approaches, such as in multimedia presentations that integrate music and drawing, can cater to both auditory and visual learners. For example, a presentation on the water cycle might feature a background song describing each stage, coupled with animations that visually depict the process. This multi-sensory approach enhances engagement and comprehension by presenting information in multiple formats, supporting diverse learning styles.

Benefits of Applying Humor and Mnemonics

Humor and mnemonic devices are powerful tools that can make learning more memorable and enjoyable, particularly in diverse classrooms. They cater to various learning preferences, ensuring that each student can grasp and retain essential information effectively.

Encouraging student participation and using humor can make content more accessible in the classroom. For instance, starting a lesson with a humorous story related to the topic can capture attention and make the material more relatable. When learning is linked to positive experiences, students are more likely to engage and retain information.

Mnemonics serve as effective memory aids, helping students encode and recall information. These devices can take many forms—acronyms, visual images, rhymes—and are particularly useful for remembering complex sequences or difficult concepts. For example, the acronym "PEMDAS" (Please Excuse My Dear Aunt Sally) helps students recall the order of operations in mathematics. Such strategies simplify learning by creating easily retrievable mental associations.

Combining humor with mnemonics can further enhance memory retention. Humorous phrases or quirky acronyms can make learning more engaging and help solidify understanding. For example, teaching the process of photosynthesis with a funny rhyme or song can make the steps more memorable. The emotional response elicited by humor aids in cognitive processing, making it easier for students to store and recall information.

Practical Implementation of Creative Instructional Strategies

Effectively integrating creative instructional tools like music, drawing, humor, and mnemonics into lesson plans requires strategic planning and adaptability. Here are practical methods for utilizing these tools:

Drawing for Note-Taking: Encouraging students to illustrate key concepts as they take notes helps create a visual representation of the material, aiding retention. In a geography class, for example, students could draw maps and landmarks to reinforce their understanding of spatial relationships.

Blending Art and Music in Group Projects: Collaborative projects that combine visual and auditory elements can deepen understanding. For example, a project on ecosystems might involve creating a mural of different habitats accompanied by a song highlighting each habitat's characteristics. This approach not only strengthens understanding of the material but also fosters teamwork and creativity.

Humor in Lessons: Incorporating humor can enhance learning without detracting from educational objectives by using funny anecdotes or jokes related to the content to make lessons more engaging. For instance, a math lesson might involve a humorous story about "The Adventures of a Lost Angle," giving each angle a personality to simplify geometric concepts.

Student-Created Mnemonics: Allowing students to develop their mnemonics fosters creativity and reinforces learning. Sharing these memory aids with classmates can establish a supportive learning environment, promoting the exchange of creative strategies among students.

Activities

The following activities provide concrete examples of how these creative approaches can be applied to different grade levels:

Activities for Elementary: Focus on fundamental connections between basic concepts and sensory experiences, such as singing songs to learn the alphabet or using drawing to visualize simple math problems.

Title	**The Multiplication Tables Rap**
Grade Level	Elementary School (Grade 2)
Objective	Memorize multiplication tables from 1 to 10 through rhythm and repetition.
Materials	Simple rhythmic backing track Lyrics for multiplication tables in rap format
Procedure	Introduce a simple beat (can be clapped or played). Present the rap lyrics for one multiplication table, for example: "2, 4, 6, 8, the 2 times table's really great! 10, 12, 14, 16, keep it going, you're a math machine! 18 and 20 to end the line, now you're doing just fine!" Have students repeat the rap while keeping the beat. Gradually introduce other multiplication tables with the same rhythm. Challenge students to create their own raps for the remaining tables.
Extension	Organize a "rap battle" of multiplication tables between groups of students.

Title	**My Four Seasons Tree**
Grade Level	Elementary School (Grade 3)
Objective	Understand seasonal changes and the life cycle of plants.
Materials	Large sheets of paper Coloring supplies (crayons, markers, watercolors) Natural materials (leaves, twigs, etc.)
Procedure	At the beginning of the school year, have each student draw a large tree with four main sections (one for each season). Throughout the year, at each change of season, dedicate a lesson to observing trees in the schoolyard or a nearby park. After observation, students update the corresponding section of their tree, drawing: • Spring: buds, flowers, new leaves • Summer: green leaves, growing fruits • Fall: colored leaves, ripe fruits • Winter: bare branches, possible snow Encourage students to add details like animals or insects typical of each season. At the end of the year, discuss the observed changes and how they affect the surrounding ecosystem.
Extension	Create a class collage combining parts of all students' drawings to form a "super tree" of the four seasons.

Activities for Middle School: Encourage more complex and autonomous exploration of abstract concepts. Projects might include creating a comic strip to explain a scientific process or composing a rap about historical events.

Title	**Fractions in Music**
Grade Level	Middle School (Grades 6)
Objective	Understand and visualize fractions through musical notation.
Materials	Whiteboard with staff lines Percussion instruments (if available) Cards with various musical notes
Procedure	Introduce basic musical notes (whole note, half note, quarter note, eighth note) and explain how they represent fractions of time. Show how a whole note (1 whole) can be divided into 2 half notes (1/2), 4 quarter notes (1/4), or 8 eighth notes (1/8). Have students create short rhythmic sequences using different musical notes, calculating the total fraction of time occupied. Ask students to clap the rhythms they've created, physically feeling the different fractions of time. Introduce concepts like addition and subtraction of fractions using combinations of musical notes.
Extension	Create a class composition where each student contributes one measure, then calculate the total fraction of the composition occupied by each student's contribution.

Title	**Solar System Mind Map**
Grade Level	Middle School (Grades 6-8)
Objective	Understand the structure of the solar system and the characteristics of planets.
Materials	Large sheets of paper or poster boards Coloring supplies (colored pencils, markers) Ruler and compass
Procedure	Introduce the concept of mind mapping and show some examples. Have students draw the Sun at the center of their paper. Starting from the Sun, draw the orbits of the planets, roughly respecting relative distances. For each planet, create a "bubble" connected with a line, where students will draw and note: • The planet's appearance (colors, rings, etc.) • Relative sizes • Composition (rocky, gaseous) • Unique features (e.g., Jupiter's storms, Saturn's rings) • Any major moons • Add sections for other celestial bodies like asteroids and comets. Encourage the use of colors and symbols to make the map visually appealing and easy to memorize.
Extension	Organize a "space art gallery" where students present and explain their mind maps to classmates.

Activities for High School: Engage in sophisticated applications that link creativity with in-depth analysis and understanding. Examples include using digital tools to create a multimedia presentation on economic theories or developing a collaborative research project that includes visual, auditory, and written components.

Title	**Trigonometric Functions and Sound Waves**
Grade Level	High School (Grades 9-10)
Objective	Visualize and understand trigonometric functions through sound waves.
Materials	Computer with sound synthesis software (e.g., Audacity, available for free) Audio speakers Graphs of trigonometric functions
Procedure	Introduce the concept of sound waves and their graphical representation. Show how sinusoidal waves correspond to the sine function in mathematics. Use the software to generate pure tones (sinusoidal waves) at different frequencies. Have students listen to different tones while simultaneously showing the corresponding graphs. Explore concepts such as amplitude (volume), frequency (pitch), and phase, linking them to transformations of trigonometric functions. Challenge students to "draw" simple melodies by modifying sound wave parameters and observing how the graphs change.
Extension	Introduce the concept of Fourier series, showing how complex waves (like the sound of an instrument) can be decomposed into a series of sinusoidal waves.

Title	**Cell Division Storyboard**
Grade Level	High School (Grades 10-11)
Objective	Visualize and understand the phases of mitosis and meiosis.
Materials	11x17 inch paper (or A3 size) Pencils and erasers Coloring supplies (colored pencils or markers) Ruler
Procedure	Divide the 11x17 inch paper into 8 equal panels. In the first 4 panels, students will draw the phases of mitosis: Prophase, Metaphase, Anaphase, Telophase In the next 4 panels, they will draw the phases of meiosis, highlighting the differences from mitosis. For each phase, students must: Accurately draw the arrangement of chromosomes and other cellular structures Label the main parts (nuclear membrane, centrioles, mitotic spindle, etc.) Add brief explanatory notes on the ongoing processes Use different colors to highlight homologous chromosomes and track their movement through the phases. At the end, discuss in class the differences between mitosis and meiosis, using the storyboards as visual references.
Extension	Create a digital animated version of the storyboard using presentation software or GIF-making apps.

By integrating these creative strategies, educators can create a more inclusive and engaging learning environment for diverse student needs.

Chapter 6

Fostering Social Interaction in the Classroom

Creating an inclusive and dynamic classroom environment hinges on the ability to foster meaningful social interactions among students. In this chapter, we delve into various strategies and activities designed to enhance social skills, collaboration, and community-building in line with the principles of UDL. By promoting engagement through structured social activities, educators can facilitate a learning atmosphere where every student feels seen, heard, and valued.

This chapter outlines practical approaches for implementing small-group activities that encourage teamwork and peer learning. It also explores the role of games and role-playing scenarios in enhancing communication skills and social awareness. Teachers will gain insights into forming diverse groups, assigning roles for balanced participation, and using peer feedback and reflection as tools for growth. Additionally, this chapter provides guidelines for designing inclusive games that foster positive social interactions and collaborative problem-solving. Through these methods, educators can nurture crucial social skills that are essential for academic success and personal development.

Implementing Small-Group Activities

Small-group activities serve as a cornerstone for fostering social interaction in the classroom. They promote collaboration and communication, allowing students to work closely with their peers, share diverse perspectives, and develop essential interpersonal skills.

To maximize the effectiveness of small-group activities, it is crucial to form groups that are diverse in terms of skills, experiences, and backgrounds. **Heterogeneous grouping** enables students to learn from each other, leveraging their diverse strengths. For example, pairing a student with strong analytical skills with one who excels in creative thinking can lead to more innovative solutions to a problem. Such diversity also encourages empathy and understanding as students engage with peers from different cultural or socioeconomic backgrounds.

Assigning specific roles within each group can further enhance participation and accountability. Roles such as **Leader, Note-taker, Researcher, and Presenter** provide structure and clarity, ensuring that every student has a defined contribution. For instance, the Leader may facilitate discussions and keep the group focused while the Researcher gathers information relevant to the task. These roles help distribute responsibility and encourage active engagement from all group members, fostering a sense of ownership and collaboration.

Incorporating **peer feedback** into group activities enhances the learning experience and fosters critical thinking and communication skills.. Using structured methods, such as the "two stars and a wish" technique—where students mention two positive aspects and one area for improvement—can create a supportive environment where students feel comfortable sharing their thoughts.

Reflection periods post-activity are equally important for consolidating learning. These sessions provide an opportunity for students to evaluate their experiences, identify strengths, and recognize areas for improvement. For example, after completing a group project, a reflection session might involve discussing questions like, "What strategies helped your group work effectively?" and "How could communication have been improved?" Such discussions encourage metacognition and self-assessment, which are critical for personal and academic growth.

Guidelines for Effective Small-Group Activities

To create diverse and effective groups, consider students' academic strengths, learning styles, and backgrounds. Regularly rotating groups allow students to interact with different peers, enhancing the learning experience and fostering a more inclusive environment. Clear communication of roles and responsibilities is crucial. Use visual aids or role cards to help students understand their tasks during activities, ensuring everyone is on the same page.

Structuring feedback sessions with specific guidelines and prompts can help students provide meaningful feedback. For example, using sentence starters like "I appreciated when you..." or "I think the group could improve by..." can guide students in articulating their thoughts constructively. Reflection can be fostered through a variety of methods, such as journaling, group discussions, or self-assessment checklists. Allowing students to choose their reflection method increases engagement and offers diverse perspectives on their experiences.

By implementing these strategies, small-group activities can significantly enhance students' social interaction, collaboration, and communication skills. They offer a dynamic and interactive learning environment that extends beyond traditional instructional methods, providing practical experiences in teamwork, empathy, and effective communication.

Using Games to Sharpen Social Interactions

Games are a versatile tool for fostering social skills and team dynamics in the classroom. They create a fun and engaging environment while promoting cooperation, communication, and inclusivity. Games encourage students to interact meaningfully, share responsibilities, and build trust, making them an excellent strategy for enhancing social interaction.

Introducing **collaborative games** that require teamwork is an effective way to promote positive social behavior and trust among peers. Sure, here is the rewritten text with corrections:

Activities such as "Capture the Flag" or "Team Building Puzzles" require students to collaborate towards a common goal, promoting a sense of community and teamwork. For instance, in the game "Human Knot," students work together to untangle themselves without letting go of each other's hands, which encourages problem-solving and teamwork.

Inclusive game design ensures that all students, regardless of their abilities, can participate meaningfully. Adapting games to suit diverse needs is crucial for creating a supportive environment.
For instance, adapting "Musical Chairs" to a seated version where students pass an object around instead of moving can make the game accessible to those with mobility challenges. Similarly, providing visual aids or simplified instructions can help students with learning disabilities participate fully.

Role-playing scenarios in games allow students to practice social interactions and enhance communication skills. These activities enable students to explore different social situations and experiment with various responses in a controlled setting. For instance, in "The Empathy Game," students assume roles of characters facing specific challenges and must navigate these scenarios by communicating and negotiating with their peers. This practice enhances empathy, perspective-taking, and social problem-solving.

Guidelines for Effective Game-Based Learning

When introducing games, it is crucial to explain the rules clearly and ensure that all students understand their roles and objectives. Establishing ground rules for respectful behavior and cooperation sets a positive tone and encourages inclusive participation. Teachers should assess the needs of their students and adapt games to ensure accessibility for all.

Role-playing scenarios should be selected based on relevance and appropriateness for the students' age group. Providing clear instructions and setting boundaries helps maintain a focused and respectful environment. Post-activity **debriefing** sessions are essential for reflecting on the experience and reinforcing lessons learned about teamwork, communication, and social strategies. Asking open-ended questions like "What did you learn about cooperation during the game?" encourages thoughtful discussion and critical reflection.

Social Activities for Fostering Interaction

Collaborative Story Circle

- Objective: Enhance creativity, listening skills, and teamwork.
- Description: Students sit in a circle. One student begins a story, and each subsequent student adds a sentence, building on the previous contributions. Roles like "Narrator" or "Detail Adder" ensure diverse participation.
- Reflection: After the story is complete, discuss how students built upon each other's ideas and the challenges faced in collaborative storytelling.

Diversity Puzzle

- Objective: Promote understanding of diverse perspectives and problem-solving skills.
- Description: Divide the class into small groups and give each group a puzzle. Each member has a unique "ability" (e.g., can only touch pieces, can only give verbal instructions). Groups must complete the puzzle by leveraging each member's strengths.
- Adaptation: Use tactile puzzles for visually impaired students or digital puzzles for those with motor challenges.

Empathy Role-Play Scenarios

- Objective: Develop empathy and communication skills through role-play.
- Description: Students are assigned roles and scenarios that require them to navigate social situations and resolve conflicts.
- Debriefing: Reflect on the different perspectives and strategies used during role-play, discussing the importance of empathy and effective communication.

Trust-Building Obstacle Course

- Objective: Foster trust, communication, and teamwork.
- Description: Set up a simple obstacle course. Students work in pairs; one is blindfolded while the other provides verbal guidance to navigate the course.
- Adaptation: Use a tabletop version for students with mobility issues.
- Debriefing: Discuss the importance of trust and clear communication in achieving goals.

Collaborative Mind Mapping

- Objective: Enhance collaborative thinking and idea organization.
- Description: In small groups, students create a mind map on a central topic, with each member contributing in a different color.
- Adaptation: Use digital mind-mapping tools for those who prefer typing or have difficulty with handwriting.

By integrating these social interaction strategies and activities, educators can create a classroom environment that not only supports academic learning but also fosters essential social skills. The diverse approaches presented here align with UDL principles, ensuring that every student has the opportunity to engage, collaborate, and thrive.

Resources

Collaborative Story Circle
https://usdac.us/storycircles

Team Building Diversity Games:
https://teambuilding.com/blog/diversity-games

Empathy Exercises and Games:
https://teambuilding.com/blog/diversity-games

Trust Building Activities: https://parenting.firstcry.com/articles/10-fun-trust-building-activities-for-kids/
https://www.indeed.com/career-advice/career-development/trust-building-activities

Collaborative Mind Mapping:
https://www.mindomo.com/blog/collaborative-mind-mapping/

Chapter 7

Developing Executive Function Skills

Executive function skills are essential for students to manage their learning processes and daily activities effectively. These skills include planning, organization, time management, and self-regulation, enabling students to approach academic challenges and tasks systematically. By fostering these abilities, educators can create a learning environment that promotes independence and helps students reach their full potential. Integrating UDL principles provides structured tools and strategies tailored to diverse learning needs, further supporting the development of executive function skills.

In this chapter, we explore practical techniques for enhancing students' executive function skills. The focus will be on the use of **templates, rubrics, graphic organizers, and timers**—tools that provide clarity, reduce cognitive load, and foster self-regulation. We will also discuss how these tools can be employed collaboratively to enhance teamwork and peer support, ultimately empowering students to take control of their learning.

Using Templates and Rubrics for Structure

Templates and rubrics are critical for helping students develop executive function skills. These tools provide a clear structure that minimizes confusion and anxiety, allowing students to focus on the learning process rather than procedural uncertainties.

Consistency and Clarity with Templates

Templates create a **consistent framework** for assignments and tasks, which is particularly beneficial in reducing the cognitive load on students. When students are familiar with the structure of a task, they can allocate more mental resources to content rather than format. For instance, a standardized template for writing assignments ensures all students approach the task with the same expectations, allowing them to concentrate on developing their ideas rather than navigating varying formats.

Templates also alleviate anxiety associated with open-ended tasks. Providing a structured outline or scaffold guides the student's thinking process, helping them overcome the intimidation of a blank page. For example, a template that outlines the sections of a lab report (introduction, method, results, discussion) provides a clear starting point and roadmap, reducing hesitation and encouraging productive writing.

Rubrics as Tools for Self-Regulation

Rubrics complement templates by providing specific criteria for success, offering students a transparent understanding of what is expected. When rubrics are provided at the start of an assignment, they serve as a roadmap for quality work. For example, a rubric that specifies what constitutes an "excellent" thesis statement or the "adequate" use of evidence allows students to self-assess their progress, making adjustments before final submission.

Immediate feedback is another significant advantage of rubrics. By self-assessing their work against the rubric criteria, students can identify areas of strength and opportunities for improvement in real-time. This approach fosters a **growth mindset**, emphasizing continuous improvement over static grading. Moreover, rubrics ensure that feedback from teachers is more targeted and constructive, focusing on specific areas rather than generalized comments.

Promoting Incremental Progress

Templates facilitate **incremental progress** by breaking down larger tasks into smaller, manageable sections. This approach helps students tackle complex projects piece by piece, reducing overwhelm and promoting a sense of accomplishment. For instance, a research paper template might be divided into stages: topic selection, preliminary research, outline creation, drafting, and revision. Each stage is a step toward the final goal, allowing students to monitor their progress and adjust their approach as needed.

By promoting incremental progress, templates also support the development of **self-regulation skills**. Students learn to manage their workflow, set mini-deadlines, and evaluate their performance against these benchmarks. This practice is invaluable beyond the classroom, where most tasks require similar planning and execution skills.

Collaborative Benefits

Using templates and rubrics in a collaborative setting enhances their utility. Consistent templates ensure all group members understand the task format and expectations, which is crucial for effective teamwork. In group projects, this alignment reduces confusion and promotes seamless collaboration.

Rubrics serve as a **mutual reference** point for peer evaluation, fostering a common language for discussing each other's work. For example, during peer review, students can use specific rubric criteria to provide constructive feedback, enhancing the quality of their reviews and deepening their understanding of the assignment requirements. This process encourages reflection on their work and reinforces learning.

Collaborative use of templates and rubrics also promotes **communication and consensus-building**. Group members must agree on how to interpret rubric criteria and divide tasks according to the template, fostering negotiation skills essential for teamwork. Additionally, working within a structured framework encourages students to support each other, share resources, and leverage collective strengths for mutual success.

Incorporating Graphic Organizers and Timers

Graphic organizers and timers are effective tools for enhancing students' executive function skills by helping them visualize tasks, organize information, and manage time effectively.

Graphic Organizers for Visual Planning

Graphic organizers are powerful aids for **visualizing and organizing** information. They help students break down complex concepts into smaller, more manageable parts. For instance, a mind map allows students to organize ideas around a central theme, visually representing the relationships between different pieces of information. This process aids comprehension and retention by making abstract concepts more concrete.

Graphic organizers are also valuable for **task management**. They enable students to decompose large projects into smaller, actionable steps, reducing overwhelm and promoting a structured approach. For example, a flowchart outlining the stages of a science experiment—hypothesis formulation, method design, data collection, analysis, and conclusion—provides a clear visual roadmap, helping students stay organized and focused.

Timers for Time Management

Timers are essential for developing time management skills, creating a sense of urgency, and helping students maintain focus. Techniques such as the Pomodoro Technique, which involves working in focused intervals with short breaks, encourage sustained concentration and prevent burnout. For example, a student might use a timer to allocate 25 minutes to complete a set of math problems, followed by a 5-minute break. This method promotes efficient use of time and helps students develop a rhythm for studying and completing tasks.

To maximize effectiveness, both graphic organizers and timers should be **customized** to individual student needs. Different learners may benefit from different types of organizers (e.g., Venn diagrams, story maps, flowcharts) or timer settings based on their attention spans. Teachers should introduce various tools and demonstrate their use in different contexts, such as using a flowchart to outline a historical event's cause and effect or a Venn diagram to compare and contrast two literary characters.

Implementation and Practice

Incorporating these tools into daily routines requires thoughtful implementation and practice. Teachers can model their use during classroom activities, showing students how to structure their study sessions or break down tasks using graphic organizers. Regular practice in both academic and everyday contexts—such as planning a weekend schedule—helps students internalize these skills, making them second nature.

Creating a supportive environment is also critical. Classrooms should be equipped with various graphic organizers and accessible timers, and space should be provided for students to display their organizers, fostering a sense of ownership and accountability. By regularly incorporating these tools, educators help students develop habits that enhance their executive function skills and independence.

.

Cognitive Mapping Aids

Analysis Template

Analysis Templates guide students through the process of systematically examining and interpreting information. These tools are invaluable in developing critical thinking and analytical skills across disciplines.

- **Structure and Guidance**: Templates provide a structured format that organizes thoughts and prompts students to focus on key aspects of the subject matter.
- **Skill Development**: They foster critical thinking, analytical reasoning, and organizational skills by providing a consistent approach to analysis.
- **Versatility**: Adaptable for various subjects, from literature to science, supporting differentiation and scaffolding learning.

An Event Analysis Template provides a comprehensive framework for examining historical events. It encourages a deep, multifaceted understanding by guiding students through a systematic examination of key factors such as causes, consequences, primary sources, and historical interpretations.

Template Components:
- **Date and Location**: Establishes the event's temporal and spatial context.
- **Key Figures**: Identifies the main individuals involved and their roles.
- **Causes and Consequences**: Explores contributing factors and impacts.
- **Long-term Impact**: Assesses the event's broader historical significance.

- **Primary Sources and Interpretations**: Encourages engagement with historical evidence and historiography.
- **Personal Reflection**: Prompts critical thinking and connections to contemporary issues.

1. Date and Location:	• When did the event occur? • Where did it take place?
2. Key Figures:	• List the main people involved • Brief description of their roles
3. Causes:	• What led to this event? • List at least three contributing factors
4. Course of Events:	• Provide a chronological summary of what happened • Include key decisions and actions
5. Immediate Consequences:	• What were the short-term effects? • How did it impact different groups of people?
6. Long-term Impact:	• How did this event influence future developments? • Discuss its significance in broader historical context
7. Primary Sources:	• List at least two primary sources related to this event • Explain what these sources reveal about the event
8. Historical Interpretations:	• How have historians' views on this event changed over time? • Discuss any controversies or debates surrounding the event
9. Personal Reflection:	• What is your opinion on the significance of this event? • How does it relate to current events or issues?
10. References:	• List all sources used in your research

Event Analysis Template

Concept Maps and Flowcharts

Concept Maps and **Flowcharts** are visual tools that facilitate knowledge organization and process visualization. They help students understand relationships between concepts and steps in a procedure.

- **Concept Maps**: Illustrate connections between ideas, enhancing comprehension of complex relationships in subjects like science or history.
- **Flowcharts**: Break down procedures into manageable steps, aiding in understanding processes in fields such as mathematics or engineering.

In **art history**, concept maps can be particularly useful for:
- Visualizing Artistic Movements: Mapping the key characteristics, influential artists, and historical context of various art movements.
- Tracing Artistic Influences: Illustrating the connections between artists, their predecessors, and their contemporaries.
- Contextualizing Artworks: Linking individual pieces to their broader historical, social, and cultural contexts.
- Comparing Styles and Techniques: Creating visual comparisons of different artistic styles, techniques, and mediums across periods.
- Exploring Thematic Evolution: Tracing the development of specific themes or motifs throughout art history.

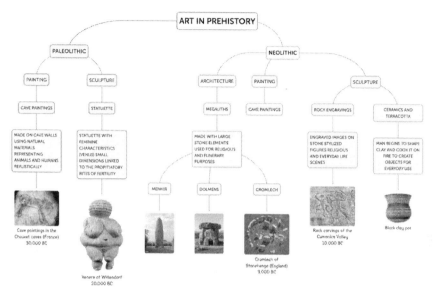

Art in Prehistory Concept Map

Flowcharts are graphical representations that utilize symbols and arrows to demonstrate the sequence of steps in a process or decision-making scenario. In education, flowcharts fulfill several purposes:

- **Simplification of Complex Processes**: They break down complicated procedures into manageable steps, making them easier for students to understand and follow.
- **Visual Learning Support**: Flowcharts cater to visual learners by presenting information in a graphical format, enhancing comprehension and retention.
- **Problem-Solving Skills Development**: They encourage students to think logically and systematically about problem-solving processes.
- **Decision-Making Practice**: Flowcharts help students understand and practice decision-making by clearly showing the consequences of different choices.

- **Concept Mapping**: They can be used to map out concepts and their relationships, aiding in the organization and connection of ideas.
- **Procedural Knowledge Reinforcement**: Flowcharts are excellent for teaching and reinforcing step-by-step procedures in various subjects.

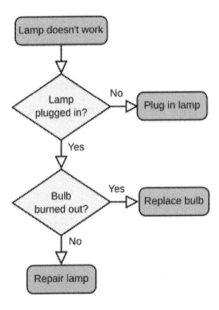

Flowchart example

A **Venn diagram** is a visual tool used to illustrate logical relationships between different sets or groups of items. It consists of overlapping circles or shapes, with each representing a set and the overlapping areas representing commonalities between sets.
Key functions of Venn diagrams include:

- **Comparison**: Illustrating similarities and differences between groups.
- **Organization**: Sorting information into distinct categories.
- **Problem Solving**: Identifying overlapping characteristics or solutions.

- **Logical Reasoning**: Visualizing set theory concepts and Boolean logic.

This Venn diagram helps students visualize the similarities and differences between two significant historical events with two overlapping circles. The left circle is labeled "American Revolution", the right circle is labeled "French Revolution", and the overlapping section represents shared characteristics.

American Revolution

French Revolution

- Occurred from 1765-1783
- Led by wealthy landowners and merchants
- Sought independence from British rule
- Resulted in a federal republic
- Maintained existing social hierarchies
- Less radical social changes

- Inspired by Enlightenment ideals
- Fought against perceived tyranny and oppression
- Emphasized liberty, equality, and popular sovereignty
- Had international impact and influence
- Led to significant political and social changes
- Resulted in the creation of new governmental systems

- Occurred from 1789-1799
- Led by the bourgeoisie and lower classes
- Sought to overthrow the monarchy and aristocracy
- Resulted in significant social upheaval
- Abolished feudalism and privileges of nobility
- More radical and violent in nature

Mind Maps and Word Clouds

Mind Maps and **Word Clouds** offer alternative visual strategies for organizing information.

- **Mind Maps**: Use a radial layout to organize information around a central concept, promoting creative thinking and idea generation.
- **Word Clouds**: Visualize word frequency and importance, providing a quick overview of key themes or concepts.

Mind Maps

Mind maps are **radial diagrams** used to organize information around a central concept visually. Unlike concept maps, which focus on showing the relationships between ideas, mind maps are more free-form and hierarchical, branching out from a central topic to subtopics and details.

Benefits of using mind maps:

- Quickly brainstorm and organize ideas;
- Visualize the scope of a topic and its various aspects;
- Enhance memory recall through visual association;
- Facilitate creative thinking and idea generation.

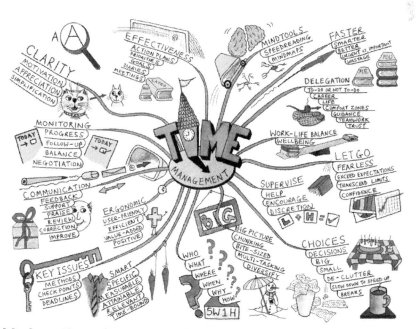

Mind map Example

Word Cloud

A Word Cloud is a graphical representation of word frequency that displays the most prominent words in a given text or concept. Unlike traditional mind maps, Word Clouds do not show hierarchical relationships but instead emphasize the relative importance of words through size and color.

Key features of Word Clouds:

- **Visual Impact**: Words are displayed in various sizes, with larger fonts indicating higher frequency or importance.
- **Shape Customization**: Words can be arranged to fill predefined shapes, adding an extra layer of visual meaning.
- **Quick Overview**: Provides an instant visual summary of key terms or concepts.
- **Versatility**: This can be generated from various text sources, including documents, speeches, or social media content.

Word Clouds are particularly useful for:

- Summarizing the main themes in a text
- Highlighting frequently used terms in a dataset
- Creating visually appealing representations of concepts
- Identifying trends in textual information

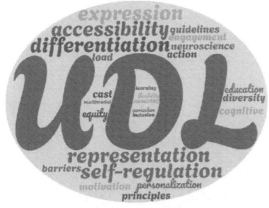

Word Cloud Example

By integrating structured tools such as templates, rubrics, graphic organizers, and timers, educators can effectively support the development of executive function skills. These strategies promote clarity, reduce cognitive load, and foster self-regulation, empowering students to manage their learning more independently. By implementing these strategies within the UDL framework, we can build a truly inclusive and supportive learning environment, empowering every student to reach their full potential!

Online Resources

Lessons Plan and Analysis Template

TeachersPayTeachers (https://www.teacherspayteachers.com):
An online marketplace where teachers share, sell, and buy original educational resources. Many educators upload analysis templates for various subjects.

ReadWriteThink (http://www.readwritethink.org):
Sponsored by the National Council of Teachers of English, this site offers a wide range of free resources, including analysis templates for language and literature teaching.

National Science Teaching Association (NSTA)
(https://www.nsta.org):
The NSTA site often provides templates and resources for scientific analysis that are suitable for various grade levels.

National Council of Teachers of Mathematics (NCTM)
(https://www.nctm.org): T
his site offers resources for teaching mathematics, including potential mathematical analysis templates.

Smithsonian Education (https://www.si.edu/educators):
The Smithsonian provides free educational resources, which may include analysis templates for history, science, and art.

PBS LearningMedia (https://www.pbslearningmedia.org):
This platform offers free educational resources, including potential analysis templates, for a wide range of subjects.

Education World (https://www.educationworld.com):
A website offering a variety of resources for teachers, including templates and tools for analysis in different disciplines.

Share My Lesson (https://sharemylesson.com):
A platform from the American Federation of Teachers that allows teachers to share resources, including potential analysis templates. Assessment Rubrics

iRubric (https://www.rcampus.com/indexrubric.cfm)
Provides a rubric development tool and a library of shared rubrics across multiple disciplines.

AAC&U VALUE Rubrics (https://www.aacu.org/value-rubrics)
Provides rubrics for assessing various learning outcomes in higher education across different disciplines.

TeachersFirst
(https://www.teachersfirst.com/lessons/rubrics/index.cfm)
Offers a collection of rubrics and rubric generators for various subjects and grade levels.

ReadWriteThink
(https://www.readwritethink.org/search?s=rubric)
Provides rubrics and assessment tools specifically for language arts and literacy.

Graphic Organizers

Coggle (https://coggle.it)
A collaborative mind mapping tool that allows real-time collaboration. Great for creating branching hierarchies and color-coded mind maps.

MindMeister (https://www.mindmeister.com)
An online mind-mapping tool that supports collaboration and integration with project management tools. Offers templates for various subjects.

Cmap Tools (https://cmap.ihmc.us)
A free tool specifically designed for creating concept maps. It's widely used in educational settings and supports cross-platform use.

Draw.io (https://app.diagrams.net)
A free diagramming tool that can be used to create flowcharts, Venn diagrams, and other types of visual organizers. It integrates with various cloud storage services.

Popplet (http://popplet.com)
A tool for creating mind maps and concept maps. It's particularly user-friendly and suitable for younger students.

Creately (https://creately.com)
Offers templates and tools for creating various types of diagrams, including mind maps, concept maps, and flowcharts. It has a specific focus on visual collaboration.

Canva (https://www.canva.com/graphs)
While known for general design, Canva offers templates for mind maps, concept maps, and Venn diagrams that can be easily customized.

Miro (https://miro.com/education-whiteboard)
An online collaborative whiteboard platform that offers templates for mind maps, concept maps, and other visual organizers.

Bubbl.us (https://bubbl.us)
A simple, web-based tool for creating colorful mind maps and brainstorming diagrams.

MindMup (https://www.mindmup.com)
A free online mind mapping tool that allows for easy creation and sharing of mind maps. It also offers a Gold version with additional features.

Gliffy (https://www.gliffy.com)
A diagramming tool that offers templates for flowcharts, Venn diagrams, and concept maps. It integrates well with team collaboration tools.

Argor (https://www.algoreducation.com)
An educational platform that offers tools for creating mind maps, concept maps, and other graphic organizers. Specifically designed to support learning and teaching, Argor features real-time collaboration and integration with other educational resources.

Xmind (https://www.xmind.net)
A mind mapping and brainstorming tool that offers various chart structures, including fishbone charts and logic charts.

Stormboard (https://stormboard.com)
An online brainstorming and collaboration tool that allows for the creation of mind maps and other visual organizers in a shared, virtual workspace.

Time Management

RescueTime (https://www.rescuetime.com)
Automatically tracks time spent on various digital activities, helping students identify and reduce distractions.

Forest App (https://www.forestapp.cc)
An app that encourages focus by allowing users to "plant virtual trees" while studying.

MyStudyLife (https://www.mystudylife.com)
A digital planner designed specifically for students, which keeps track of classes, assignments, and exams.

Trello (https://trello.com)
A project management platform that can be used to organize tasks and collaborate on group projects.

Evernote (https://evernote.com)
A note-taking app that helps students organize information and manage deadlines.

Pomodoro Timer (https://pomofocus.io)
An online timer based on the Pomodoro Technique which helps break study time into manageable intervals.

Cal Newport's Study Hacks Blog
(https://www.calnewport.com/blog)
A blog offering advanced strategies for time management and effective studying.

Khan Academy - College Admissions
(https://www.khanacademy.org/college-careers-more/college-admissions)
Offers free resources on time management and organization for students preparing for college.
Clockify (https://clockify.me)
A free time tracker that can help students monitor how much time they spend on different activities.

Notion (https://www.notion.so)
An all-in-one platform for notes, task management, and collaboration, popular among students.

Asana (https://asana.com)
A project management tool that can be used to organize individual or group tasks.

StudyBlue (https://www.studyblue.com)
A platform for creating flashcards and study materials, which also includes tools for study time management.

GoConqr (https://www.goconqr.com)
Offers tools for creating mind maps, flashcards, and quizzes, as well as resources for managing study time.

Habitica (https://habitica.com)
An app that turns task management into a role-playing game, motivating students to complete tasks.

Chapter 8

Assessing Student Learning

Assessment in education is most effective when it aligns with the UDL principles. Traditional methods like standardized tests and quizzes often need to capture the full range of a student's understanding and abilities. Instead, innovative assessment techniques that offer **flexibility and inclusivity** provide a more accurate reflection of student learning. By diversifying assessment formats and incorporating technology, educators can create environments where all learners are empowered to demonstrate their knowledge in ways that align with their strengths.

This chapter outlines various UDL-aligned assessment techniques, focusing on **adapted tests, collaborative projects, and formative assessments**. We will explore how to design assessments that accommodate different learning styles, utilize assistive technologies, and integrate family collaboration, fostering a deeper connection between home and school. These strategies aim to create a more equitable and engaging assessment environment that meets the diverse needs of all students.

Designing Adapted Tests and Quizzes

Creating adapted assessments is crucial for supporting diverse learners. These assessments are developed to accommodate different learning styles, preferences, and needs, ensuring that every student has the opportunity to effectively demonstrate their knowledge and skills.

Flexible Question Formats

Incorporating multiple question formats within the same assessment—such as multiple-choice, short answer, and performance tasks—allows students to engage with the content in ways that suit their strengths. This diversity reduces anxiety and fosters a more inclusive assessment environment. For example, a student who excels in verbal explanations but struggles with written tasks might perform better on an assessment that includes an option to give an oral presentation. Similarly, performance tasks, such as demonstrations or practical applications, allow students to showcase their understanding in a hands-on manner, which can be particularly beneficial for kinesthetic learners.

Scaffolding Questions

Scaffolding is a technique that involves breaking down complex questions into smaller, more manageable parts. This approach helps students gradually build their understanding and confidence. For instance, rather than asking a broad question like, "Explain the causes and effects of the Industrial Revolution," a scaffolded approach might begin with, "Identify three major changes that occurred during the Industrial Revolution." Subsequent questions could then explore how these changes impacted society, politics, and economics. Scaffolding ensures that students can engage with complex topics more effectively, leading to deeper learning and better assessment outcomes.

Leveraging Assistive Technologies

Assistive technologies play a crucial role in creating inclusive assessments. Tools such as speech-to-text software, text-to-speech applications, and digital magnification tools can significantly support students with disabilities, allowing them to engage fully in assessments.

For example, a student with dyslexia might use text-to-speech software to understand written questions better, while a student with motor difficulties might use speech-to-text tools to compose their responses. These technologies ensure equitable access for all students.

Formative assessments are ongoing, informal evaluations that provide immediate feedback to students and teachers. Unlike summative assessments, formative assessments allow for continuous monitoring and adjustment of teaching strategies to meet student needs better. Examples include quizzes, class discussions, and peer reviews. Regular, constructive feedback helps students recognize areas for improvement and develop strategies to enhance their learning.

Examples of Adapted Assessment Tools

Adaptation Type	Description
Multiple Response Formats	Traditional written tests Oral exams Video presentations Hands-on demonstrations Digital quizzes with multimedia elements
Extended Time	Providing 1.5x or 2x the standard time for test completion Allowing tests to be completed over multiple sessions
Text-to-Speech and Speech-to-Text	Using software that reads test questions aloud Allowing students to dictate their answers
Visual Aids	Including diagrams, charts, or images to supplement text Allowing students to respond with drawings or concept maps
Simplified Language	Rewording complex questions without changing the core concept being tested Providing a glossary of terms used in the test
Flexible Settings	Allowing students to take tests in a quiet room Permitting movement breaks during long exams
Assistive Technology	Allowing use of calculators or formula sheets Permitting screen readers or magnification software
Alternative Question Types	Replacing essay questions with short answer or multiple choice Using true/false questions with explanations
Portfolio Assessments	Evaluating a collection of student work over time instead of a single test
Project-Based Assessments	Allowing students to demonstrate knowledge through practical projects
Chunking Information	Breaking long tests into smaller, more manageable sections
Choice in Assessment	Allowing students to choose how they want to be assessed (e.g., written report, oral presentation, or practical

Method	demonstration)
Use of Manipulatives	Providing physical objects for math or science assessments
Collaborative Assessments	Allowing peer-to-peer explanations or group projects as assessment methods
Digital Tools	Using online platforms that allow for personalized test settings (font size, color contrast, etc.)

Implementing Family Projects for Collaborative Assessment

Family projects are an innovative approach to assessment that fosters collaboration between home and school. By engaging families in project-based learning (PBL), teachers can create meaningful assessment opportunities that extend beyond the classroom. This method encourages families to participate actively in their child's education, transforming assessments into shared, experiential learning opportunities.

Project-Based Learning with Family Involvement

Incorporating Project-Based Learning as an assessment strategy allows students to collaborate with family members on projects that reinforce classroom learning. For example, a science project on recycling could involve parents and siblings in researching waste management practices, creating a home recycling plan, and presenting findings. This hands-on approach deepens understanding and makes learning more relevant by connecting academic concepts to real-life experiences.

Culturally Responsive Assessments

Culturally responsive assessments recognize and celebrate the diverse cultural backgrounds of students. By incorporating elements of students' cultures into assessments, teachers can create more meaningful and inclusive learning experiences. For instance, a social studies project might encourage students and their families to explore their cultural heritage and present their findings through a family artifact, a traditional recipe, or an oral history. This not only validates students' cultural identities but also enriches classroom discussions with diverse perspectives.

Reflection and Feedback

Reflection and feedback are integral to effective assessment. Encouraging students and families to reflect on their project experiences fosters deeper understanding and personal growth. A post-project discussion where families share what they learned, what they enjoyed, and what they found challenging helps solidify the learning experience. Teachers can facilitate this reflection by providing prompts and guiding questions, such as "What was the most surprising thing you learned?" or "How did this project change your understanding of the topic?"

Feedback from peers and teachers during these projects can also be valuable. Constructive feedback encourages students to think critically about their work and identify areas for improvement. When feedback is part of a supportive and collaborative environment, students are more likely to embrace it as a tool for growth.

Showcasing Projects

Opportunities to showcase projects strengthen the connection between home and school, fostering a sense of community and pride. Family nights, classroom displays, or virtual exhibitions allow students to present their projects, share their learning, and celebrate their achievements with peers, teachers, and family members. These events create an inclusive atmosphere where all contributions are valued, promoting a positive learning environment.

Guidelines for Effective Implementation

Clear guidelines and expectations are essential to successfully implementing family projects. Teachers should provide detailed instructions, including project goals, timelines, and suggested roles for family members. Flexibility is also important, as families have different resources, schedules, and levels of engagement. Offering various options for participation ensures that all families can be involved in ways that suit their circumstances.

Continuous communication with families throughout the project is crucial for maintaining engagement and addressing challenges. Regular updates and check-ins, facilitated through newsletters, classroom apps, or virtual meetings, help keep families informed and involved. This ongoing dialogue fosters a collaborative partnership between home and school, enhancing the overall educational experience for students.

By incorporating **innovative, inclusive assessment techniques**, educators can create a more equitable and engaging learning environment that recognizes and celebrates the diverse abilities and strengths of all students. Utilizing adapted tests, collaborative projects, formative assessments, and family involvement, teachers can provide meaningful opportunities for all students to demonstrate their learning and achieve their fullest potential.

Resources

Assessment Tools

Quizlet (https://quizlet.com)
Platform offering flashcards, games, and study modes with text-to-speech support for accessibility.

Kahoot! (https://kahoot.com)
Interactive quiz platform supporting multiple question types and self-paced assessments.

Google Forms (https://www.google.com/forms/about/)
Customizable survey and quiz tool that integrates well with assistive technologies.

Nearpod (https://nearpod.com)
Interactive lesson and assessment platform incorporating VR and 3D objects.

Formative (https://www.formative.com)
Real-time assessment tool allowing multiple response types, including text, audio, video, and drawing.

Edulastic (https://edulastic.com)
Customizable assessment platform with over 70 tech-enhanced question types and special needs accommodations.

Socrative (https://www.socrative.com)
Assessment tool featuring quick questions and game-like activities for individual and team evaluations.

Pear Deck (https://www.peardeck.com)
Interactive presentation and assessment tool integrated with Google Slides and Microsoft PowerPoint.

Flipgrid (https://info.flipgrid.com)
Video discussion platform enabling students to respond to prompts through short videos.

ClassKick (https://classkick.com)
Digital workspace for assignments and assessments with real-time teacher feedback capabilities.

Seesaw (https://web.seesaw.me)
Digital portfolio and assessment platform supporting various file types for student responses.

Edpuzzle (https://edpuzzle.com)
Tool for creating interactive video lessons with embedded assessment questions.

Plickers (https://get.plickers.com)
Assessment tool using printed cards and a mobile device, suitable for classrooms with limited technology.

Mentimeter (https://www.mentimeter.com)
Interactive presentation software with built-in assessment features like word clouds and scales.

Padlet (https://padlet.com) Digital bulletin board for collaborative assessments, supporting text, images, links, and files.

Google Read&Write (https://www.texthelp.com/products/read-and-write-education/)
Comprehensive literacy support tool offering both Text-to-Speech and Speech-to-Text functionalities.

Natural Reader (https://www.naturalreaders.com/)
Text-to-Speech tool capable of reading assessment questions aloud to students.

Dragon NaturallySpeaking

(https://www.nuance.com/dragon.html)
Powerful Speech-to-Text tool enabling students to dictate their assessment responses.

Microsoft Immersive Reader

(https://education.microsoft.com/en-us/resource/9b010288)
The tool offers both text-to-speech and dictation features, along with additional reading supports.

Chapter 9

Creating UDL Lesson Plans

As we move from theory to practice in our exploration of Universal Design for Learning, we now turn our attention to the crucial task of creating effective UDL lesson plans. This process involves not just designing learning experiences but also integrating ongoing assessment to ensure our teaching remains responsive and effective.

The heart of a UDL lesson plan lies in its **flexibility and inclusivity**. Rather than aiming for a one-size-fits-all approach, we strive to create multi-faceted learning experiences that offer multiple pathways for students to engage with content, represent their understanding, and express their knowledge.

In this chapter, we'll guide you through the process of creating a UDL lesson plan that not only incorporates the three core principles but also weaves in effective formative assessment strategies. We'll explore how to **design activities** that provide immediate feedback, allow for self-assessment, and inform our instructional decisions.

We'll also consider how to integrate **Howard Gardner's Theory of Multiple Intelligences** into our planning. This theory, which proposes eight different types of intelligence (linguistic, logical-mathematical, spatial, musical, bodily-kinesthetic, interpersonal, intrapersonal, and naturalistic), aligns well with UDL's emphasis on diverse learning approaches. By addressing these various intelligences, we can further enhance the inclusivity and effectiveness of our teaching.

Remember, creating UDL lesson plans is an **iterative process**. As you implement these plans and gather formative assessment data, you'll continually reflect on their effectiveness and make necessary adjustments. This ongoing cycle of planning, teaching, assessing, and adapting is at the core of responsive, student-centered instruction.

In the following sections, we'll break down the steps to create a comprehensive UDL lesson plan, providing practical examples and tips along the way. By the end of this chapter, you'll have the tools and confidence to design lessons that truly cater to the diverse needs of your classroom, guided by ongoing assessment and feedback.

Step-by-Step UDL Lesson Plan

Step 1: Define Clear Learning Objectives

Start by clearly defining what you want your students to learn. Your objectives should be specific, measurable, achievable, relevant, and time-bound (SMART). Consider the following:

- What key concepts should students understand by the end of the lesson?
- What skills should they be able to demonstrate?
- How does this lesson fit into the broader curriculum?

Example: "By the end of this two-week unit, students will be able to identify, represent, and compare fractions using visual, numerical, and real-world examples."

Step 2: Consider Multiple Means of Engagement

Think about how you can motivate and engage all learners. UDL focuses on offering choices for self-regulation, maintaining effort and perseverance, and engaging interest. Consider:

- How can you connect the content to students' interests and real-world applications?
- What choices can you offer students in terms of learning activities?
- How can you provide opportunities for collaboration and individual work?

Example activities:
A "Fraction Hunt" where students find real-world examples of fractions.
Interactive digital games that teach fraction concepts.
A collaborative art project incorporating fractions.

Step 3: Plan for Multiple Means of Representation

Offer information in more than one format. This helps learners access content in ways that best suit their learning styles. Consider:

- How can you present the information visually, auditorily, and kinesthetically?
- What digital tools or manipulatives can support understanding?
- How can you connect new information to students' prior knowledge?

Example activities:
Creating a physical or digital "Fraction Flipbook" for visual learners.
Using virtual manipulatives to explore fraction concepts.
Watching instructional videos with closed captions.

Step 4: Design for Multiple Means of Action and Expression

Provide diverse ways for students to express what they know. This allows students to demonstrate their understanding in ways that work best for them. Consider:

- What options can you provide for physical action?
- How can students use various media to express their learning?
- What tools can assist students in their learning and demonstration of knowledge?

Example activities:
Creating a "Fraction Quilt" as a hands-on, collaborative project.
Producing a digital e-book about fractions.
Performing a skit or song that explains fraction concepts.

Step 5: Develop a Comprehensive Assessment Plan
Create a rubric that assesses understanding while allowing for diverse expressions of knowledge. Your assessment should:

- Align with your learning objectives
- Accommodate different learning styles and abilities
- Provide opportunities for self-assessment and reflection

Example: A rubric that evaluates understanding of fractions, artistic representation, engagement, collaboration, and use of digital tools.

Step 6: Map Activities to Multiple Intelligences
Consider Howard Gardner's theory of Multiple Intelligences when planning your activities. Ensure that your lesson engages a range of intelligences, such as:

- Linguistic (word smart)
- Logical-mathematical (number/reasoning smart)
- Spatial (picture smart)
- Bodily-Kinesthetic (body smart)
- Musical (music smart)
- Interpersonal (people smart)
- Intrapersonal (self smart)
- Naturalistic (nature smart)

Step 7: Plan for Necessary Resources and Accommodations
Identify the resources needed for your lesson, including:

- Physical materials (e.g., art supplies, manipulatives)
- Digital tools and platforms
- Any necessary accommodations for students with specific needs

Step 8: Review and Refine

After creating your UDL lesson plan, review it to ensure:

- All three UDL principles (Engagement, Representation, Action & Expression) are addressed
- Activities are varied and cater to diverse learning needs
- The plan is flexible and allows for adjustments based on student responses

Generic UDL Lesson Plan Template

The lesson plans presented in this book follow a consistent and intentional structure, carefully designed to integrate UDL principles and meet diverse learning needs. Each lesson plan is designed to provide a comprehensive learning experience that aligns with the UDL framework, emphasizing engagement, representation, action, and expression. The structure ensures that educators can easily adapt and implement lessons based on grade levels, subject matter, and student abilities. Here, we provide a generic outline as a guideline.

1. Lesson Information

Each lesson begins with a concise overview that includes the following key components:

Grade Level: Specifies the target grade level range for the lesson (e.g., 3rd-4th grade), ensuring that the content is developmentally appropriate.

Subject Areas: Identifies the major subject areas covered in the lesson (e.g., math, art), highlighting cross-curricular connections where applicable.

Duration: Provides an estimate of the length of the lesson, typically structured to fit a standard class period (e.g., 1 hour).

Theme: Outlines the central theme or focus of the lesson (e.g., exploring geometry and shapes), providing a thematic anchor around which the activities are centered.

Objective: Clearly state the learning objectives, specifying what students are expected to understand and accomplish by the end of the lesson (e.g., understanding and identifying basic geometric shapes and their properties through mathematics and art).

Details	Content
Grade Level	Specify grade level (e.g., K-12, 3rd Grade, etc.)
Disciplines	List the subject(s) involved (e.g., Mathematics, Art, History)
Duration	Total time for the lesson (e.g., 1 hour, 2 weeks)
Theme	Describe the central theme of the lesson (e.g., "Exploring Geometry and Shapes")
Objective	Clearly state the learning objectives (e.g., "Understand and identify basic geometric shapes and their properties through mathematics and art.")

2. Description

This section provides a narrative overview of the lesson, summarizing the key activities and pedagogical strategies employed. It provides context for how the lesson integrates UDL principles and accommodates various learning styles. The description explains how digital and analog tools are used to enhance learning, as well as how different activities are sequenced to build on each other, promoting a deep understanding of the topic.

Description
Provide a brief description of the lesson, detailing the overarching goals and how various activities align with the principles of Universal Design for Learning. Include how the lesson caters to multiple learning styles and preferences, and mention any interdisciplinary connections.

3. Lesson Structure

The lesson structure is outlined in a step-by-step format, detailing the sequence of activities along with their time allocations. Each activity is designed to align with one or more UDL principles, ensuring a balanced approach to engagement, representation, action, and expression. The structure typically includes:

Time: A clear time allocation for each activity (e.g., 0-10 min), helping teachers manage class periods effectively.

Activity: The name of the activity (e.g., Intro to Shapes), which provides a snapshot of what students will be doing.

Description: A brief explanation of the activity, including the learning objectives it addresses and the teaching methods used (e.g., a brief overview of basic shapes and their properties, using real-life examples to connect geometry to everyday life).

Materials/Tools: Lists the resources needed for each activity, including digital (e.g., tablet, computer) and analog (e.g., whiteboard, cut-out shapes), ensuring teachers are well-prepared to teach the lesson.

UDL Principle (UDL Prin.): Specifies which UDL principles each activity addresses using. Abbreviations used:

- Engagement (E)
- Representation (R)
- Action and Expression (AE).

Often, you will find multiple principles combined (e.g., "E+R" indicates that Engagement and Representation are incorporated).

Time	Activity	Description	Materials/Tools	UDL Prin
0-10 min	Introduction to [Topic]	Introduce the main concepts related to the topic using engaging visual aids and real-life examples to connect the content to students' experiences.	Whiteboard, projector, images, or models	R
10-20	Exploration:	Utilize digital tools or	Tablets/computers	E +

min	[Interactive or Digital]	interactive activities to explore deeper concepts related to the topic, encouraging hands-on digital learning and visual engagement.	with internet access, specific software or applications	R
20-30 min	[Hands-on or Collaborative Activity]	Engage students in a hands-on or group activity that reinforces concepts through tactile or collaborative methods, fostering kinesthetic and interpersonal learning.	Physical materials (e.g., manipulatives, paper, markers), group activity guides	AE
30-40 min	[Creative or Reflective Activity]	Incorporate creativity into learning through activities that blend the arts with the subject content or provide a reflective practice that deepens understanding.	Art supplies (e.g., colored paper, scissors, glue), or reflective journals, digital platforms for sharing thoughts	AE + E
40-50 min	[Discussion or Critical Thinking]	Facilitate a guided discussion or critical thinking exercise that encourages students to analyze and synthesize information, fostering higher-order thinking skills.	Discussion guides, projector, or interactive whiteboard	R + AE
50-60 min	Reflection and E-Portfolio Creation	Conclude with a reflective exercise where students document their learning journey using digital portfolios or reflective journals, reinforcing digital literacy and self-assessment skills.	Tablets/computers with internet access, e-portfolio platform (e.g., Seesaw)	AE

4. Assessment Rubric

To support a UDL approach to assessment, each lesson plan includes a detailed rubric that provides clear criteria for assessing student performance.

The rubric is designed to accommodate different ways of demonstrating understanding and mastery, aligning with UDL principles. It typically consists of:

Criteria: Defines the specific skills or areas of knowledge assessed (e.g., form identification, artistic integration, participation, and engagement).

Performance Levels: Describes various levels of proficiency:

- 4 (Excellent)
- 3 (Good)
- 2 (Satisfactory)
- 1 (Needs Improvement)

Provides qualitative descriptors for each level to guide both teachers and students in understanding the expectations.

Points (Pt.): Assigns point values to each criterion, supporting both formative and summative assessment practices.

Criterion	4	3	2	1	Pt.
[Knowledge Skill Area]	Shows deep understanding and accurate application of the content or skills.	Demonstrates good understanding with minor errors or omissions.	Basic understanding with some errors or gaps in application.	Limited understanding with significant errors or omissions.	/10
[Application in Activities]	Effectively applies knowledge in all activities, showing strong	Applies knowledge in most activities with reasonable engagement	Limited application of knowledge in activities, with minimal	Struggles to apply knowledge; lacks engagement in activities.	/10

	engagement and creativity.	.	engagement .		
[Collaboration Participation]	Works exceptionally well in groups, contributing effectively to the group's success.	Generally works well in groups, contributing adequately.	Somewhat cooperative, but limited in contributing to group activities.	Rarely participates or contributes to group activities.	/10
[Use of Digital Tools]	Masterfully integrates digital tools to enhance learning and demonstrate understanding.	Adequately uses digital tools with some level of understanding.	Uses digital tools, but with limited understanding or effectiveness.	Struggles to use digital tools effectively, with minimal output.	/10
[Reflective Creative Skills]	Provides insightful reflections or highly creative outputs that demonstrate deep understanding.	Reflects adequately or creates with some clarity and creativity.	Provides basic reflections or creative outputs with limited depth.	Minimal reflection or creativity, showing little understanding.	/10

5. UDL Activity Grid

The UDL Activity Grid provides a visual representation of how different activities align with UDL principles. It provides a quick reference for teachers, highlighting both digital and analog activities that accommodate different learning styles. The grid typically includes:

UDL Principle (UDL Prin): Indicates the UDL principle that each activity supports (E, R, AE).

Activity: Name the activity (e.g., Interactive Geometry Tool, Shape Collage).

Description: Briefly describe the activity and how it engages, represents, or enables the expression of knowledge.

Delivery: Specifies whether the activity is digital or analog, allowing for flexibility in lesson delivery.

Platform/Tool: Lists any specific platforms or tools required (e.g., GeoGebra, Google Arts & Culture).

UDL Prin	Activity	Description	Delivery	Platform/Tool
E	[Interactive Digital Activity]	Engages students through digital tools that allow for exploration and interactive learning.	Digital	[e.g., Specific Software or App]
E+R	[Visual and Auditory Presentation]	Combines visual and auditory learning through videos or multimedia presentations to cater to multiple sensory modalities.	Digital or Analog	[e.g., Projector, Audio System, Video Platform]
R	[Foundational Knowledge Delivery]	Provides a foundation of knowledge using clear visual aids, diagrams, and direct instruction to build understanding.	Analog Digital	[e.g., Whiteboard, Projector, Visual Aids]
AE	[Hands-on or Creative Exercise]	Involves students in tactile or creative activities that foster active expression and manipulation of concepts.	Analog	[e.g., Craft Materials, Digital Creation Tools]
AE+E	[Collaborative Problem-Solving]	Encourages students to work in groups or pairs to solve problems or create products, enhancing engagement and collaboration.	Digital or Analog	[e.g., Collaborative Software, Group Activity Sets]

6. Multiple Intelligences Table

To further align with UDL and accommodate different learning preferences, each lesson plan includes a table that maps activities to Howard Gardner's Multiple Intelligences. This ensures that the lesson takes into account various strengths and intelligences, such as linguistic, logical-mathematical, spatial, bodily-kinesthetic, musical, interpersonal, intrapersonal, and naturalistic. The table includes:

Intelligence: The type of intelligence (e.g., linguistic, spatial).

Activity: The related activity (e.g., geometry vocabulary flashcards, making shapes with straws).

Description: How the activity develops or uses that particular intelligence.

Intelligence	Activity	Description
Linguistic	[Reading/Discussion-Based Activity]	Enhances linguistic intelligence through reading, writing, and discussion-based activities.
Logical-Mathematical	[Problem-Solving/Analysis Activity]	Engages logical-mathematical intelligence by involving students in problem-solving and analysis exercises.
Spatial	[Visual/Spatial Exploration]	Develops spatial intelligence through activities involving visual-spatial reasoning and manipulation.
Bodily-Kinesthetic	[Physical Manipulation Task]	Engages bodily-kinesthetic intelligence through movement-based or hands-on activities.
Musical	[Integration of Music/Rhythm]	Enhances musical intelligence by integrating music or rhythm into learning experiences.
Interpersonal	[Group Collaboration Activity]	Promotes interpersonal intelligence through collaborative group activities and peer interactions.
Intrapersonal	[Reflective Journaling]	Develops intrapersonal intelligence through self-reflection and personal goal-setting activities.
Naturalistic	[Environment-Based Learning]	Engages naturalistic intelligence by connecting learning to the natural environment or real-world contexts.

Practical Applications of UDL Lesson Plans

Geometry and Shapes (Elementary School)

Lesson Information	Details
Grade Level	3rd-4th Grade
Disciplines	Mathematics, Art
Duration	4 hours
Theme	Exploring Geometry and Shapes
Objective	Understand and identify basic geometric shapes and their properties through mathematics and art.

Description

This lesson on geometry and shapes fosters a comprehensive understanding of basic geometric concepts. The session opens with an introduction to fundamental shapes—circles, squares, triangles, and rectangles—where students learn to identify and describe their properties. Real-life examples are used to make geometry relatable, showing its relevance in everyday contexts.

Next, students engage with GeoGebra, an interactive tool that allows them to manipulate shapes, observing how their properties change with resizing and rotation. This digital activity enhances understanding by allowing students to experiment with geometric concepts in a dynamic, visual format, promoting hands-on digital learning.

The lesson then shifts to a tactile shape-sorting activity, where students categorize cutouts based on properties like the number of sides and angles. This hands-on approach reinforces earlier concepts and supports kinesthetic learning, aiding in the internalization of geometric properties.

Art integration comes through a shape collage, encouraging students to create images using cut-out shapes. This activity merges creativity with geometry, helping students understand how shapes fit together in a cohesive design while enhancing fine motor skills and spatial reasoning.

A group geometry puzzle fosters collaboration, requiring students to work together to fit shapes into a specific design. This reinforces problem-solving skills, teamwork, and spatial awareness.

The lesson concludes with students creating a digital portfolio on Seesaw, where they document their learning through reflections and images. This not only reinforces their understanding but also enhances digital literacy and provides a modern method of assessment. The blend of interactive, tactile, and creative activities ensures a rich, engaging learning experience that caters to various learning styles.

127

Lesson Structure

Time	Activity	Description	Materials/Tools	UDL Prin
0-10 min	Introduction to Shapes	Brief overview of basic shapes (circle, square, triangle, rectangle) and their properties. Use real-life examples to connect geometry to everyday life.	Whiteboard, markers, shape cutouts	R
10-20 min	Interactive Geometry Tool	Students use GeoGebra to explore and manipulate geometric shapes, observing changes in properties as shapes are resized or rotated.	Tablets/computers with internet access	E
20-30 min	Shape Sorting Activity	Students sort physical cutouts of shapes into categories based on their properties, such as number of sides and angles.	Shape cutouts, sorting trays	R
30-40 min	Shape Collage (Art Integration)	Create a collage using cut-out shapes from colored paper. Students arrange the shapes to form a picture or pattern, focusing on how shapes fit together.	Colored paper, scissors, glue	AE
40-50 min	Group Geometry Puzzle	In groups, students solve a puzzle where they must fit shapes together to form a specific design or picture.	Geometry puzzle sets	E
50-60 min	Reflection and E-Portfolio Creation	Students use Seesaw to create a digital portfolio where they upload pictures and reflections on the shapes they learned about.	Tablets/computers with internet access	AE

Assessment rubric

Criterion	4	3	2	1	Pt.
Identification of Shapes	Accurately identifies all shapes and explains properties well.	Identifies most shapes accurately, with correct property details.	Identifies some shapes correctly, with limited property details.	Struggles to identify shapes; few or no correct properties noted.	/10
Art Integration	Creatively integrates shapes into art, with a clear rationale.	Integrates shapes into art, with an adequate explanation.	Uses shapes in art, but with a basic explanation.	Limited use of shapes in art, with minimal or unclear explanation.	/10
Participation and Engagement	Highly engaged; contributes thoughtfully in all activities.	Generally engaged; participates in most activities.	Somewhat engaged; minimal participation in activities.	Rarely engaged; little to no participation.	/10
Use of Digital Tools	Masterfully uses digital tools to explore and create shapes.	Adequately uses digital tools with some creativity.	Uses digital tools, but with limited creativity or understanding.	Struggles to use digital tools effectively.	/10
Collaboration	Works exceptionally well with peers, fostering group success.	Works well with peers, contributing to group tasks.	Somewhat cooperative, but limited contribution to group success.	Rarely works cooperatively; little to no contribution to the group.	/10

UDL Activities Grid

UDL Prin	Activity	Description	Delivery	Platform/Tool
E	Interactive Geometry Tool	Students explore shapes on GeoGebra, manipulating them to see how their properties change with size and rotation.	Digital	GeoGebra
	Shape Hunt	A classroom or schoolyard "shape hunt" where students search for and identify geometric shapes in their environment.	Analog	Physical environment
	Shape Collage	Creating a collage with colored paper, focusing on how different shapes fit together to form a picture or pattern.	Analog	Colored paper, scissors, glue
	Virtual Art Gallery	Exploring artwork that prominently features geometric shapes on Google Arts & Culture, followed by group discussions.	Digital	Google Arts & Culture
R	Video Lesson on Shapes	Students watch a video introducing basic geometric shapes and their properties, with real-life examples.	Digital	Khan Academy
	Shape Sorting Activity	Sorting physical shape cutouts into categories based on their properties, like number of sides and angles.	Analog	Shape cutouts, sorting trays
	Geometry Vocabulary Flashcards	Creating flashcards with shapes on one side and their properties on the other to quiz each other.	Analog	Flashcards
	Interactive Geometry Quiz	An online quiz where students match shapes to their names and properties.	Digital	Quizlet
AE	Shape Construction with Straws	Using straws and connectors to construct 3D shapes, describing their edges, vertices, and faces.	Analog	Straws, connectors
	Digital Art Project	Using Tinkercad to design a 3D model incorporating various geometric shapes, then presenting to the class.	Digital	Tinkercad
	Group Geometry Puzzle	Solving a geometry puzzle in groups, fitting shapes together to form a specific design or picture.	Analog	Puzzle sets

	E-Portfolio of Shapes	Creating a digital portfolio on Seesaw to showcase learning progress, including pictures, drawings, and reflections on geometric shapes.	Digital	Seesaw

Multiple Intelligence Table

Intelligence	Activity	Description
Linguistic	Geometry Vocabulary Flashcards	Enhances linguistic intelligence through learning and using geometric terminology.
Logical-Mathematical	Interactive Geometry Tool	Engages logical-mathematical skills by manipulating and understanding geometric shapes.
Spatial	Shape Construction with Straws	Develops spatial awareness and visual-spatial intelligence by constructing 3D shapes.
Bodily-Kinesthetic	Shape Hunt	Engages bodily-kinesthetic intelligence by moving around and identifying shapes in the environment.
Musical	Shape Patterns in Music	Explores the relationship between geometric shapes and patterns in music, such as rhythm and beats.
Interpersonal	Group Geometry Puzzle	Enhances interpersonal intelligence through collaborative puzzle-solving activities.
Intrapersonal	E-Portfolio of Shapes	Develops intrapersonal intelligence by reflecting on learning and progress in a digital portfolio.
Naturalistic	Shape Hunt in Nature	Connects geometry with the natural world by identifying shapes found in nature.

U.S. Geography and Natural Resources (Middle School)

Lesson Information	Details
Grade Level	6th-7th Grade
Disciplines	Geography, Economics
Duration	4 hours
Theme	Exploring the Relationship Between U.S. Geography and Natural Resources
Objective	Analyze how the geographical features of the United States influence the distribution and use of natural resources and understand the economic impact of these resources.

Description

This lesson plan aims to explore the relationship between U.S. geography and the distribution of natural resources, highlighting their economic significance.

The lesson begins with an introduction to the major geographical regions of the United States. This overview focuses on the differences in climate, terrain, and natural resources across these regions.

Following this, students engage in an exploration activity where they map the distribution of key natural resources across the United States. Using either physical or digital maps, they examine how geography influences the location of resources such as coal, oil, timber, and agricultural products.

In the next phase, students work in small groups to research the economic impact of specific natural resources on different U.S. regions. Each group focuses on a particular resource and investigates how these resources contribute to the regional economy. They then present their findings to the class, highlighting the importance of these resources and the economic activities they support.

The lesson continues with an interactive simulation that allows students to manage natural resources in a fictional region of the U.S. They must make decisions balancing resource extraction with environmental sustainability and economic needs.

A discussion on the impact of geography on resource use follows. The debate also covers challenges such as environmental degradation and economic dependency on certain resources.

The lesson concludes with a reflection and sharing session, where students reflect on what they have learned about the connection between U.S. geography and natural resources. They discuss how this knowledge can be applied to make informed decisions about resource use in their communities, promoting a deeper understanding of the importance of responsible resource management.

Lesson Structure

Time	Activity	Description	Materials/Tools	UDL Prin
0-10 min	Introduction to U.S. Geography	Begin with an overview of the major geographical regions of the United States, including the Rocky Mountains, Great Plains, Appalachians, and coastal areas. Discuss how these regions differ in terms of climate, terrain, and resources.	Map of U.S. regions, projector, whiteboard	R
10-20 min	Exploration: Mapping Natural Resources	Students explore and map the distribution of key natural resources across the United States, such as coal in the Appalachians, oil in Texas, and wheat in the Midwest. Discuss how geography influences where these resources are found.	Physical or digital maps, access to National Geographic Resource Map, projector	R+E
20-30 min	Group Activity: The Economics of Natural Resources	In small groups, students research how specific natural resources contribute to the economy of a particular region (e.g., timber in the Pacific Northwest, agriculture in the Midwest). Each group presents their findings, focusing on how these resources are used and their economic importance.	Access to digital archives, research tools, presentation software (e.g., Google Slides), projector	AE+E
30-40 min	Interactive Simulation: Resource Management	Students participate in a simulation where they manage the use of natural resources in a fictional region of the U.S. They must make decisions about how to balance resource extraction with environmental sustainability and economic needs.	Online simulation tool (e.g., EcoKids Interactive Games), computers/tablets	AE+E
40-50 min	Discussion: The Impact of Geography on Resource Use	Lead a discussion on how geographical features shape the way natural resources are used and managed in the United States. Explore the challenges of resource extraction, such as	Discussion guides, projector	R+E

		environmental degradation and economic dependency on certain resources.		
50-60 min	Reflection and Sharing	Students reflect on what they learned about the connection between U.S. geography and natural resources. They share their thoughts on how this knowledge can help in making informed decisions about resource use in their own communities.	Classroom discussion, reflection journals	R+AE

Assessment **Rubric**

Criterion	4	3	2	1	Pt.
Understanding of U.S. Geography	Demonstrates a deep understanding of the geographical regions of the U.S. and effectively connects these regions to the distribution of natural resources.	Shows a good understanding of U.S. geography with mostly accurate connections to the distribution of natural resources.	Demonstrates a basic understanding of U.S. geography, with some errors or missing connections to the distribution of natural resources.	Limited understanding of U.S. geography, with significant inaccuracies or missing connections to the distribution of natural resources.	/10
Mapping and Geographical Skills	Effectively uses maps to analyze the distribution of natural resources across the U.S., demonstrating clear understanding of geographical influences.	Uses maps with some understanding, making basic connections between geography and the distribution of natural resources.	Uses maps with limited insight, making few connections between geography and the distribution of natural resources.	Struggles to use maps effectively, with minimal connections between geography and the distribution of natural resources.	/10
Group Presentation on Economic Impact	Presents a well-researched and thoughtful analysis of	Presents a good analysis of the economic impact of natural	Presents a basic analysis of the economic impact of natural	Presentation is incomplete or lacks significant detail on the	/10

	the economic impact of natural resources in a specific U.S. region, showing a deep understanding of their importance.	resources, with some detail and accuracy in connecting them to the region.	resources, with limited detail or accuracy in connecting them to the region.	economic impact of natural resources in the region.	
Participation in Simulation Activity	Actively participates in the resource management simulation, demonstrating an understanding of how to balance resource use with sustainability and economic needs.	Participates in the simulation with some understanding, managing decisions and exploring outcomes effectively.	Participates in the simulation with limited understanding or engagement, struggling to make informed decisions.	Minimal participation in the simulation, with little to no understanding of the balance between resource use and sustainability.	/10
Reflection and Presentation Skills	Provides insightful reflections on the connection between U.S. geography and natural resources, presenting ideas confidently and clearly.	Reflects adequately on the connection between U.S. geography and natural resources, presenting ideas with some clarity and confidence.	Provides a basic reflection with limited clarity or confidence in presenting ideas.	Minimal reflection and unclear presentation of ideas, showing little understanding of the material.	/10

135

UDL Activities Grid

UDL Prin	Activity	Description	Delivery	Platform/Tool
E	Exploration: Mapping Natural Resources	Students engage with the distribution of natural resources by exploring maps, learning how geography influences where resources are found across the U.S.	Analog Digital	Physical or digital maps, access to National Geographic Resource Map, projector
	Interactive Simulation: Resource Management	Students participate in a simulation that challenges them to manage natural resources sustainably, making learning interactive and reflective.	Digital	Online simulation tool (e.g., EcoKids Interactive Games), computers/tablets
R	Introduction to U.S. Geography	Use visual aids, maps, and images to introduce students to the key geographical regions of the U.S. and their associated natural resources, providing a foundational understanding of their economic significance.	Analog Digital	Map of U.S. regions, projector, whiteboard
	Discussion: The Impact of Geography on Resource Use	Students discuss how geographical features shape the way natural resources are used and managed, focusing on challenges such as environmental degradation and economic dependency.	Analog	Discussion guides, projector
AE	Group Activity: The Economics of Natural Resources	Students research and present on the economic impact of natural resources in a specific U.S. region, using digital platforms to organize and share their findings.	Digital	Access to digital archives, research tools, presentation software (e.g., Google Slides), projector
	Reflection and Sharing	Students reflect on the connection between U.S. geography and natural resources, sharing their insights through discussion and written reflections.	Analog	Classroom discussion, reflection journals

Multiple Intelligences Table

Intelligence	Activity	Description
Linguistic	Reflection and Discussion	Develops linguistic intelligence through reflecting on and discussing the connection between U.S. geography and natural resources.
Logical-Mathematical	Geographical Mapping and Analysis	Enhances logical-mathematical intelligence by analyzing maps and understanding how geography influences the distribution of natural resources.
Spatial	Visual Analysis and Mapping	Enhances spatial intelligence by exploring maps and visual representations of natural resources across the U.S., connecting geography to economic factors.
Bodily-Kinesthetic	Simulation and Group Work	Engages bodily-kinesthetic intelligence through hands-on activities like participating in the resource management simulation and collaborating in group presentations.
Musical	Optional: Exploring Sounds of Resource-Rich Environments	Explore how the natural sounds of different U.S. regions reflect the environments where natural resources are found, engaging musical intelligence by connecting geography to auditory experiences.
Interpersonal	Group Research and Presentation	Promotes interpersonal intelligence by encouraging collaboration in researching the economic impact of natural resources and presenting findings.
Intrapersonal	Reflection and Self-Assessment	Develops intrapersonal intelligence through personal reflection on the significance of natural resources and their relevance to economic development.
Naturalistic	Exploring Environmental Impact	Engages naturalistic intelligence by analyzing how resource extraction affects the environment and how geography influences these impacts.

137

Newton's Laws of Motion (High School)

Lesson Information	Details
Grade Level	9th-10th Grade
Disciplines	Physics, Mathematics
Duration	4 hours
Theme	Understanding Newton's Laws of Motion and Their Mathematical Applications
Objective	Analyze and apply Newton's three laws of motion, using mathematical equations to solve problems related to force, mass, and acceleration.

Description

This lesson plan provides a comprehensive understanding of Newton's three laws of motion. Through a blend of theoretical exploration, practical demonstrations, and problem-solving activities, the lesson aims to enhance students' grasp of how these fundamental laws govern everyday phenomena and guide them in applying mathematical equations to real-world scenarios.

The session begins with an introduction to Newton's three laws of motion, using visual aids and real-world examples to illustrate each law.

Following the introduction, students engage in a hands-on exploration of Newton's First Law of Motion. A simple classroom demonstration, such as pulling a tablecloth out from under dishes without disturbing them or using a toy car on a ramp, vividly illustrates the concept of inertia.

The lesson then shifts to a mathematical focus on Newton's Second Law. Students are introduced to the equation $F = ma$ (Force = mass $\times$ acceleration) and guided through several practice problems to apply this formula. Working individually or in pairs, they calculate the force needed to accelerate different masses.

Next, students work in small groups to create experiments demonstrating Newton's Third Law of Motion. Using materials like balloons, strings, and spring scales, they develop and present experiments that showcase action-reaction pairs.

The class then participates in a discussion on how Newton's Laws apply to everyday life, including sports dynamics, vehicle safety, and engineering. This interactive dialogue encourages students to share their observations and examples, linking theoretical concepts to practical, real-world applications.

To conclude the lesson, students reflect on what they have learned and solve complex problems that integrate all three laws of motion.

Lesson Structure

Time	Activity	Description	Materials/Tools	UDL Prin
0-10 min	Introduction to Newton's Laws of Motion	Begin with an overview of Newton's three laws of motion. Provide real-world examples for each law, such as a car accelerating (First Law), pushing a shopping cart (Second Law), and a rocket launch (Third Law).	Diagrams of real-world examples, video clips of the laws in action, projector, whiteboard	R
10-20 min	Exploration: Demonstrating Newton's First Law	Conduct a simple demonstration of inertia (First Law), such as pulling a tablecloth out from under dishes or using a toy car and ramp. Discuss how objects at rest stay at rest and objects in motion stay in motion unless acted upon by an external force.	Toy car, ramp, tablecloth, dishes, classroom materials, or Physics Classroom Interactive	R+E
20-30 min	Mathematical Application: Newton's Second Law	Introduce the equation F=ma (Force = mass × acceleration). Guide students through solving problems using this equation, such as calculating the force needed to accelerate a given mass. Provide practice problems for students to work on individually or in pairs.	Calculators, worksheets with problems, whiteboard for examples	AE+E
30-40 min	Group Activity: Newton's Third Law in Action	In small groups, students create simple experiments to demonstrate Newton's Third Law, such as balloon rockets or action-reaction pairs with spring scales. Each group presents their experiment and explains how it illustrates the Third Law.	Balloons, string, spring scales, various materials for experiments, or PhET Interactive Simulations	AE+E
40-50 min	Discussion: Connecting the Laws of Motion to Everyday Life	Lead a discussion on how Newton's Laws apply to everyday situations, such as sports, vehicle safety, and engineering. Encourage students to share examples from their own experiences and explore how understanding these laws can be useful in real life.	Discussion guides, projector	R+E

| 50-60 min | Reflection and Problem Solving | Students reflect on the concepts learned and complete a set of complex problems that require applying all three of Newton's Laws of Motion. Encourage them to work through the problems using the concepts discussed. Finish with a Q&A to clarify any remaining questions. | Reflection journals, worksheets, whiteboard | R+AE |

Assessment Rubric

Criterion	4	3	2	1	Pt.
Understanding of Newton's Laws	Demonstrates a deep understanding of Newton's three laws of motion, effectively explaining and applying them to real-world situations.	Shows a good understanding of Newton's laws with mostly accurate explanations and applications to real-world situations.	Demonstrates a basic understanding of Newton's laws, with some errors or missing connections to real-world situations.	Limited understanding of Newton's laws, with significant inaccuracies or missing connections to real-world situations.	/10
Application of Mathematical Concepts	Effectively applies the equation F=ma to solve problems, demonstrating clear understanding and accuracy.	Applies the equation F=ma with some understanding, solving problems with mostly accurate results.	Applies the equation F=ma with limited understanding, solving problems with some errors or inaccuracies.	Struggles to apply the equation F=ma, with significant errors or inaccuracies in problem-solving.	/10
Group Experiment and Presentation	Creates a well-designed experiment that effectively demonstrates Newton's Third Law, with a clear	Designs a good experiment that demonstrates Newton's Third Law, with a mostly accurate	Designs a basic experiment with limited effectiveness in demonstrating Newton's Third Law, with some	Experiment is poorly designed or ineffective in demonstrating Newton's Third Law, with significant inaccuracies	/10

	and accurate explanation during the presentation.	explanation during the presentation.	inaccuracies in the explanation.	in the explanation.	
Participation in Discussion	Actively participates in the discussion, providing thoughtful examples and connections between Newton's Laws and everyday life.	Participates in the discussion with some relevant examples and connections between Newton's Laws and everyday life.	Participates minimally in the discussion, with limited examples or connections between Newton's Laws and everyday life.	Little to no participation in the discussion, with minimal or no contribution to understanding Newton's Laws.	/10
Reflection and Problem Solving	Provides insightful reflections on Newton's Laws and successfully completes complex problems that require applying all three laws.	Reflects adequately on Newton's Laws and completes problems with some success and accuracy.	Provides a basic reflection with limited success in solving problems, with some errors or misunderstandings.	Minimal reflection and significant struggles in solving problems, with little understanding of the material.	/10

UDL Activities Grid

UDL Prin	Activity	Description	Delivery	Platform/Tool
E	Exploration: Demonstrating Newton's First Law	Students engage with Newton's First Law through a hands-on demonstration of inertia, observing how objects behave when forces are applied or removed.	Analog Digital	Toy car, ramp, tablecloth, dishes, classroom materials, or Physics Classroom Interactive
	Group Activity: Newton's Third Law in Action	Students work in groups to create and present experiments that demonstrate Newton's Third Law, making learning interactive and collaborative.	Analog Digital	Balloons, string, spring scales, various materials for experiments, or PhET Interactive Simulations
R	Introduction to Newton's Laws of Motion	Use visual aids, diagrams, and real-world examples to introduce students to Newton's three laws of motion, providing a foundational understanding of their principles.	Analog Digital	Diagrams of real-world examples, video clips of the laws in action, projector, whiteboard
	Discussion: Connecting the Laws of Motion to Everyday Life	Students discuss how Newton's Laws apply to everyday situations, sharing examples and exploring the practical applications of these principles.	Analog	Discussion guides, projector
AE	Mathematical Application: Newton's Second Law	Students apply the equation $F=ma$ to solve problems, practicing their mathematical skills and reinforcing their understanding of Newton's Second Law.	Analog	Calculators, worksheets with problems, whiteboard for examples
	Reflection and Problem Solving	Students reflect on Newton's Laws and complete a set of problems that require applying all three laws, reinforcing their understanding through practice and reflection.	Analog	Reflection journals, worksheets, whiteboard

Multiple Intelligences Table

Intelligence	Activity	Description
Linguistic	Reflection and Discussion	Develops linguistic intelligence through reflecting on and discussing Newton's Laws and their applications in everyday life.
Logical-Mathematical	Problem Solving and Mathematical Application	Enhances logical-mathematical intelligence by solving problems using Newton's Second Law and understanding the relationship between force, mass, and acceleration.
Spatial	Visual Analysis and Diagram Interpretation	Enhances spatial intelligence by analyzing diagrams and real-world examples that illustrate Newton's Laws, connecting visual information to physical concepts.
Bodily-Kinesthetic	Hands-On Demonstrations and Experiments	Engages bodily-kinesthetic intelligence through hands-on activities like demonstrating inertia and creating experiments to illustrate Newton's Third Law.
Musical	Optional: Exploring Rhythms and Forces in Music	Explore how rhythmic forces in music can be related to physical forces and motion, engaging musical intelligence by connecting physics to music.
Interpersonal	Group Work and Collaboration	Promotes interpersonal intelligence by encouraging collaboration in creating and presenting experiments that demonstrate Newton's Laws.
Intrapersonal	Reflection and Self-Assessment	Develops intrapersonal intelligence through personal reflection on the applications of Newton's Laws and their relevance to everyday life.
Naturalistic	Optional: Exploring Forces in Nature	Explore how Newton's Laws apply to natural phenomena,

Chapter 10

Transition Planning for Adulthood

Transition planning for adulthood is a critical phase in preparing students for life beyond the classroom. This chapter outlines comprehensive strategies designed to equip students with the skills and resources necessary for a successful transition into adulthood, emphasizing the importance of individualized planning and the use of UDL principles to create inclusive, student-centered pathways.

Creating Goal Plans and Transition Charts

Understanding Individual Needs

To develop effective transition plans, it is essential to conduct thorough assessments that identify each student's strengths, challenges, and aspirations. This understanding forms the foundation for creating tailored goals and strategies that align with each student's unique profile.

- **Assessments** should encompass a wide range of areas, including academic performance, social skills, career interests, and personal objectives. For example, a student who excels in visual arts but struggles with math will need a different transition plan than a student with strong analytical skills but limited social interactions.
- **Dialogue** with students is crucial to uncover these individual facets. Teachers and counselors should engage in ongoing conversations with students to better understand their interests, preferences, and aspirations, thereby creating more personalized and effective transition strategies.

Developing SMART Goals

Once individual needs are identified, the next step is to develop **SMART goals**: Specific, Measurable, Achievable, Relevant, and Time-bound. These goals provide clear direction and structure for the transition process.

- **Specific**: Clearly define what the student aims to achieve. For example, instead of a vague goal like "find a job," a specific goal would be "secure a part-time job in graphic design by the end of the school year."
- **Measurable**: Establish criteria for tracking progress, such as the number of job applications submitted or interviews attended.
- **Achievable**: Set realistic goals based on the student's current abilities and resources, avoiding targets that might lead to frustration or disengagement.
- **Relevant**: Ensure the goals are aligned with the student's broader life aspirations and values.
- **Time-bound**: Include a clear timeframe to maintain focus and urgency, such as "by the end of the school year."

Using Visual Transition Charts

Visual aids like transition charts can help simplify and clarify the steps needed to achieve SMART goals. These tools break down complex tasks into manageable components, making the transition process less daunting and providing constant visual reminders of progress and upcoming milestones.

Examples of Visual Aids:

- **Flowcharts**: Map out the steps needed to achieve a goal, showing the sequence of tasks and their dependencies.
- **Timelines**: Provide a chronological overview of tasks, helping students manage time and prioritize activities.
- **Step-by-Step Guides**: Detail specific actions needed to complete each phase of the transition, making the process more accessible and easier to follow.

For instance, a transition chart for a student aiming to attend college might include steps such as researching schools, scheduling campus visits, completing applications, and preparing for interviews. Visual aids can also highlight how the completion of one task can impact the next, encouraging students to stay organized and proactive.

Involving Families in Transition Planning

Family involvement plays a vital role in successful transition planning. Families offer crucial support and insights that can significantly enhance the student's planning and execution of transition goals.

Strategies for Family Involvement:

- **Regular Meetings**: Hold consistent check-ins with families to discuss progress and adjust plans as needed.
- **Open Communication**: Maintain transparent communication channels to ensure all parties are aligned on the student's goals and expectations.
- **Shared Responsibilities**: Encourage families to take on specific roles or tasks that support the student's transition, such as helping with job applications or exploring post-secondary education options.

By actively engaging families in the transition process, educators can create a more supportive and comprehensive network around the student, increasing the likelihood of a successful transition.

Using Real-world Applications and Projects

Integrating real-world experiences with classroom learning is crucial for developing the skills students need in adulthood. The following strategies help bridge the gap between academic knowledge and practical life skills:

Project-Based Learning (PBL)

PBL is an instructional approach that encourages students to engage with real-world problems and challenges through hands-on projects. PBL promotes critical thinking, collaboration, and the practical application of knowledge.

Example: In a high school science class, students could be tasked with designing a sustainable garden for their community. This project would require integrating biology, environmental science, and mathematics while also collaborating with local experts. As students navigate each phase of the project, they develop problem-solving skills, teamwork, and effective communication abilities.

Internships and Job Shadowing

Internships and job shadowing provide students with firsthand experience in potential careers, offering a practical understanding of workplace dynamics and expectations. These opportunities help students make informed decisions about their future paths.

Example: A student interested in healthcare could shadow a nurse or intern at a local hospital, gaining exposure to medical procedures, patient care, and the administrative aspects of healthcare. Such experiences reinforce the student's interest and highlight the skills and knowledge required for success in the field.

Community-Based Learning (CBL)

CBL involves partnerships with local organizations to undertake service-learning projects that address community needs while supporting educational objectives. CBL fosters civic responsibility and social awareness among students.

Example: An English class might collaborate with a local nonprofit to create promotional materials for a community event. This project would require students to use their writing and design skills in a real-world context, enhancing their technical abilities and understanding of effective communication and marketing.

Incorporating Technology

Leveraging **technology** is essential for preparing students for the digital age. Technologies like **Virtual Reality (VR)** and **Augmented Reality (AR)** can simulate real-world scenarios, allowing students to practice skills and make decisions in a risk-free environment.

Example: A history teacher might use VR to transport students back to significant historical events, providing a vivid and engaging learning experience. Alternatively, career exploration platforms can help students investigate various professions by offering virtual tours, interviews with professionals, and interactive assessments.

Implementing Effective Transition Strategies

To successfully implement these strategies, educators should provide clear guidelines and continuous support.

- **Project-Based Learning**: Define the project's scope, set clear objectives, and establish assessment criteria. Facilitate group dynamics and provide resources and feedback throughout the project.
- **Internships and Job Shadowing**: Ensure placements align with students' interests and prepare mentors to provide meaningful guidance.
- **Community-Based Learning**: Coordinate with community partners to design projects that meet both educational and societal goals.
- **Technology** Integration: Select appropriate tools and provide training to maximize the benefits of digital learning.

By thoughtfully implementing these strategies, educators can effectively support students in making successful transitions to adulthood, equipped with the skills and confidence they need to navigate the complexities of adult life.

Online Resources

Transition Planning for Adulthood

National Technical Assistance Center on Transition (NTACT)
(https://transitionta.org)
Provides evidence-based and promising practices for transition planning.

Center for Parent Information and Resources (CPIR)
(https://www.parentcenterhub.org/transition-starters/)
Offers resources for parents on transition planning and special education.

Wrightslaw Transition
(https://www.wrightslaw.com/info/trans.index.htm)
Offers legal information and resources on transition planning and special education law.

Think College (https://thinkcollege.net/)
Offers resources for students with intellectual disabilities transitioning to college.

National Parent Center on Transition and Employment
(https://www.pacer.org/transition/)
Provides tools and information for families and professionals on transition and employment.

Autism Speaks Transition Tool Kit
(https://www.autismspeaks.org/tool-kit/transition-tool-kit)

Offers a comprehensive guide for transition planning for individuals with autism.

Got Transition (https://www.gottransition.org/)
Focuses on health care transition from pediatric to adult care.
Project-Based Learning (PBL)

Buck Institute for Education (PBLWorks)
(https://www.pblworks.org/)
Offers comprehensive resources, professional development, and research on PBL.

Edutopia - Project-Based Learning
(https://www.edutopia.org/project-based-learning)
Provides articles, videos, and practical tips for implementing PBL.

High-Quality Project-Based Learning (https://hqpbl.org/)
Offers a framework for high-quality PBL and resources for educators.
The George Lucas Educational Foundation
(https://www.lucasedresearch.org/)
Conducts and shares research on innovative learning practices, including PBL.

New Tech Network (https://newtechnetwork.org/)
Supports schools in implementing PBL and provides resources for educators.

Magnify Learning (https://www.magnifylearningin.org/)
Provides PBL training and resources for educators and schools.

The Teachers Guild (https://www.teachersguild.org/)
Provides a collaborative platform for teachers to share and develop PBL ideas.

Cult of Pedagogy - Project-Based Learning

(https://www.cultofpedagogy.com/project-based-learning/)
Offers podcast episodes, articles, and resources on PBL.

Project Foundry (https://projectfoundry.com/)
Provides project management tools specifically designed for PBL.

Community-Based Learning (CBL)

Learning to Give (https://www.learningtogive.org/)
Offers free K-12 lesson plans and resources for teaching philanthropy, service, and civic engagement.

National Youth Leadership Council (https://www.nylc.org/)
Provides resources and training on service-learning for K-12 educators and students.

GenerationOn (https://www.generationon.org/)
Offers service-learning resources and project ideas for kids, teens, and educators.

Education World - Service Learning
(https://www.educationworld.com/a_admin/service-learning-resources.shtml)
Provides lesson plans and resources for service-learning projects in elementary and middle schools.

DoSomething.org (https://www.dosomething.org/us)
While geared towards teens, it offers ideas for community service projects adaptable for younger students.

Project Learning Tree (https://www.plt.org/)
Provides environmental education resources that often incorporate community-based learning for K-12.

Teaching Tolerance (Learning for Justice)
(https://www.learningforjustice.org/)

Offers resources for social justice education that often incorporate community engagement.

Youth Service America (https://ysa.org/)
Offers resources and project ideas for youth service and civic engagement, including for younger students.

National Geographic Education
(https://www.nationalgeographic.org/education/)
Provides resources for community-based environmental education projects.

Green Schools National Network
(https://greenschoolsnationalnetwork.org/)
Offers resources for sustainability education that often incorporate community-based learning.

Earth Force (https://earthforce.org/)
Engages young people as active citizens who improve the environment and their communities.

Campus Compact (https://compact.org/)
National coalition of colleges and universities committed to the public purposes of higher education, including CBL.

Community-Campus Partnerships for Health
(https://www.ccphealth.org/)
Promotes health equity and social justice through partnerships between communities and academic institutions.

Learn and Serve America
(http://www.nationalservice.gov/programs/discontinued-programs/learn-and-serve-america)
While discontinued, their archived resources remain valuable for CBL.

The Collaborative for Academic, Social, and Emotional Learning (CASEL) (https://casel.org/)
While focused on SEL, they provide resources that connect community engagement with social-emotional learning.

National Education Association - Community Schools
(https://www.nea.org/student-success/great-public-schools/community-schools)
Offers resources on community schools, which often incorporate CBL principles.

Coalition of Urban and Metropolitan Universities (CUMU)
(https://www.cumuonline.org/)
It focuses on urban engagement and often includes resources on CBL in urban settings.

Community Learning Network
(http://www.communitylearningnetwork.org/)
Offers resources and networking opportunities for educators interested in community-based learning.

Virtual reality (VR) and augmented reality (AR)

VirtualSpeech (https://virtualspeech.com/)
Provides VR training for public speaking and job interviews, enhancing students' professional communication skills.

Augmented Reality for Education
(https://www.arleneducation.com/)
Offers AR solutions for education, including tools that support career exploration and skill development.

ClassVR (https://www.classvr.com/)
Provides VR and AR educational content, featuring career exploration and virtual field trips to broaden students' horizons.

Labster (https://www.labster.com/)
Offers virtual lab simulations that introduce students to STEM fields and advanced scientific concepts.

Google Expeditions (https://edu.google.com/products/vr-ar/)
While primarily for general education, it offers virtual field trips that can be used for career exploration and expanding students' worldviews.

Mursion (https://www.mursion.com/)
Provides VR simulations for developing social skills and job interview practice, preparing students for professional environments.

Strivr (https://www.strivr.com/)
Offers VR-based training solutions that can be adapted for developing vocational skills and workplace readiness.

MEL Science (https://melscience.com/)
Provides AR and VR science lessons, which can deepen understanding of advanced STEM concepts.

VR Education (https://immersivevreducation.com/)
Offers educational VR experiences that familiarize students with higher education environments and academic expectations.

ThingLink (https://www.thinglink.com/)
Offers tools for creating interactive images, videos, and virtual tours, which can be used for orientation and familiarization with new environments.

Unimersiv (https://unimersiv.com/)
Provides educational VR experiences, including historical reconstructions and anatomy lessons, enhancing academic understanding across various subjects.

zSpace (https://zspace.com/)
Provides AR/VR technology for education, including applications that support career exploration and skill development in various fields.

Chapter 11

Global UDL Implementation: Case Studies and Impact Analysis

UDL has emerged as a transformative framework in education, promising to create more inclusive, effective, and engaging learning environments for all students. As educational systems worldwide grapple with the challenges of diversity, accessibility, and equity, UDL offers a flexible and comprehensive approach to curriculum design and instruction.

This short chapter delves into real-world implementations of UDL across **various global contexts**, providing concrete evidence of its impact and adaptability.

The case studies presented here span four continents and **diverse educational settings**, from elementary schools to universities, offering a panoramic view of UDL's application and effectiveness. Each case study provides valuable insights into the implementation process, the challenges encountered, and the measurable outcomes achieved. By examining these varied experiences, we can better understand the universal applicability of UDL principles as well as the need for context-specific adaptations.

Our journey begins in the United States, where we explore a district-wide implementation of UDL in secondary schools in Indiana. This case provides a longitudinal perspective on how systematic UDL integration can impact graduation rates and college readiness. We then move to Canada, focusing on elementary education, where the Three-Block Model of UDL demonstrates its efficacy in enhancing student engagement and teacher efficacy.

Crossing the Atlantic, we examine UDL's role in higher education through the lens of an Irish university's experience in health science courses. This case offers insights into UDL's potential to create more accessible learning environments in specialized academic fields. Finally, we travel to South Africa, where UDL principles are adapted to resource-limited settings, showcasing the framework's flexibility and potential in diverse socioeconomic contexts.

These case studies collectively address several critical questions:

1. How does UDL implementation vary across different educational levels and cultural contexts?
2. What are the measurable impacts of UDL on student engagement, achievement, and inclusion?
3. What challenges are commonly encountered in UDL implementation, and how are they addressed?
4. How can UDL principles be adapted to settings with limited resources?
5. What insights can these diverse implementations offer for future UDL adoptions worldwide?

By examining these real-world applications, this chapter aims to provide educators, policymakers, and researchers with a nuanced understanding of UDL's potential and challenges. It underscores the framework's capacity to address a wide range of educational needs while highlighting the importance of contextual adaptation and continuous evaluation.

As we delve into each case study, we invite readers to consider how these experiences might inform their educational practices and policies. The global nature of these examples emphasizes that while education systems may differ, the goal of creating inclusive, effective learning environments is universal. Through these diverse narratives, we can glean valuable lessons for the future of education in an increasingly interconnected and diverse world.

United States: Transforming Secondary Education in Indiana

In the heart of Indiana, the Bartholomew Consolidated School Corporation (BCSC) embarked on an ambitious journey to implement UDL across its six high schools. This initiative, which began in 2010, offers a compelling look at the long-term effects of UDL in secondary education.

The BCSC approach was comprehensive, involving **intensive teacher training** and the creation of **UDL leadership teams** in each school. These teams were instrumental in integrating UDL principles into lesson planning and daily classroom practices. The results were impressive: the graduation rate climbed from 88% in 2012 to 91.7% in 2016. Perhaps even more striking was the 300% increase in students earning college credits during high school between 2010 and 2016.

However, the path was with obstacles. Some teachers initially resisted changing their established teaching methods, and the curriculum redesign demanded a significant time investment. Despite these challenges, the overall impact on student engagement and achievement was undeniably positive.

This case demonstrates how a systematic, district-wide implementation of UDL can lead to substantial improvements in student outcomes, particularly in areas like graduation rates and college readiness.

Source: Meier, B. (2019). Universal Design for Learning Implementation in Six High Schools. ProQuest LLC.

Canada: UDL in Elementary Education

Shifting our focus to elementary education, a study in Ontario, Canada, provides valuable insights into the implementation of UDL in younger age groups. This research examined the application of the Three-Block Model of UDL in three elementary schools.

The Canadian approach focused on comprehensive teacher training in the UDL three-block model, coupled with a **redesign of learning spaces** to support inclusion. A key component was the implementation of **cooperative learning strategies**, which proved particularly effective in engaging younger students.

The results were encouraging. Teachers showed a significant increase in their use of UDL practices, with their average score rising from 2.63 to 3.30 on a 4-point scale. This quantitative improvement was accompanied by a qualitative shift in teachers' perceptions of inclusion and their teaching efficacy.

One of the most notable outcomes was the increase in students' active engagement time during lessons. This finding is particularly crucial in elementary education, where capturing and maintaining young learners' attention can be challenging.

The study also highlighted ongoing challenges, such as the need for continuous support for teachers and the complexity of balancing diverse student needs in heterogeneous classrooms. These insights are valuable for other elementary schools considering UDL implementation.

Source: Katz, J. (2013). The Three-Block Model of Universal Design for Learning (UDL): Engaging students in inclusive education. Canadian Journal of Education, 36(1), 153-194.

Ireland: UDL in Higher Education

Moving to the higher education sector, an Irish university's experience with UDL in health science courses offers a unique perspective on the framework's applicability in specialized, **professional education settings**.

The Irish implementation involved a thorough redesign of courses according to UDL principles, **extensive faculty training**, and the creation of **accessible learning materials**. This comprehensive approach addressed not just classroom teaching but the entire educational experience, including clinical placements.

The outcomes were notable: a 7% increase in course completion rates for students with disabilities and a 50% reduction in requests for individual accommodations. These figures suggest that the UDL approach was effective in creating a more inherently accessible learning environment, reducing the need for after-the-fact adjustments.

Interestingly, the study also reported improved overall student satisfaction with course accessibility. This finding indicates that UDL benefits extend beyond students with disclosed disabilities to the broader student population.

However, the implementation faced challenges, including initial resistance from some faculty members accustomed to traditional teaching methods and the need for investments in assistive technologies. These obstacles highlight the importance of change management and resource allocation in UDL implementation.

Source: Heelan, A., Halligan, P., & Quirke, M. (2015). Universal Design for Learning and its application to clinical placements in health science courses. Journal of Postsecondary Education and Disability, 28(4), 469-479.

South Africa: Adapting UDL to Resource-Limited Settings

Our final case study takes us to South Africa, where researchers examined the introduction of UDL principles in the context of **limited resources**. This study provides valuable insights into how UDL can be adapted and implemented in challenging educational environments.

The South African approach centered on conducting **workshops for teachers and therapists**, introducing UDL strategies adapted to the local context. A key focus was on creating **flexible teaching materials** with limited resources, encouraging creativity and innovation among educators.

The results showed significant improvements in teachers' understanding of UDL principles and an increased awareness of the importance of inclusive education. Perhaps most importantly, the study highlighted the development of creative strategies to implement UDL with minimal resources.

However, the challenges were substantial. Overcrowded classrooms made it difficult to implement some UDL strategies, and many schools needed more technological resources. Additionally, UDL principles need to be adapted to fit the local cultural and socioeconomic context.

This case study is particularly valuable as it demonstrates the flexibility of UDL and its potential applicability in diverse global contexts, even those facing significant resource constraints.

Source: Dalton, E. M., Mckenzie, J. A., & Kahonde, C. (2012). The implementation of inclusive education in South Africa: Reflections arising from a workshop for teachers and therapists to introduce Universal Design for Learning. African Journal of Disability, 1(1), 1-7.

These case studies collectively illustrate the global reach and adaptability of UDL. From improving graduation rates in the United States to enhancing inclusive practices in resource-limited settings in South Africa, UDL has demonstrated its potential to impact diverse educational environments positively.

While challenges persist, the overall trend suggests that UDL, when thoughtfully implemented and adapted to local contexts, can significantly enhance educational experiences and outcomes for a wide range of learners.

Chapter 12

Bringing It All Together

Reflecting on Successes and Challenges

To effectively integrate UDL strategies, educators must reflect on their current practices, identify successes, and address challenges. This reflective process is crucial for continuous improvement and fostering an inclusive learning environment.

Identifying Successes

Teachers play a vital role in creating inclusive classrooms by tailoring education to meet diverse needs. Sharing success stories within the teaching community can be a powerful tool for motivation and learning. For example, a teacher who successfully incorporates multiple means of representation—such as visual aids, auditory materials, and hands-on activities—into their lessons enables students with varied learning preferences to grasp complex concepts more effectively.

Sharing Real-World Examples

- **Multiple Means of Representation:** A science teacher might use videos, diagrams, and physical models to explain the water cycle, allowing all students, regardless of their learning style, to access the material.
- **Flexible Learning Environments:** A language arts teacher could create different reading groups based on interest and reading level, promoting engagement and comprehension.

By sharing these real-world examples, educators can see the tangible benefits of UDL integration, encouraging them to adopt similar approaches in their classrooms.

Addressing Challenges

While promoting UDL is effective, it has challenges. Common barriers include limited resources, time constraints, or resistance to change. Recognizing these difficulties is crucial for finding practical solutions.

Common Challenges and Solutions:

- **Limited Resources:** A lack of technological tools may hinder efforts to adapt materials for various learning styles. Solutions include utilizing low-cost or free resources such as open educational resources (OERs), leveraging community partnerships, or collaborating with colleagues to share materials.
- **Time Constraints:** Integrating UDL strategies can initially seem time-consuming. Streamlining lesson planning by using templates or co-creating resources with peers can reduce preparation time.
- **Resistance to Change:** Overcoming resistance involves highlighting the benefits of UDL through evidence-based practices and demonstrating its positive impact on student learning outcomes.

Developing an Assessment Framework

To ensure the effective implementation of UDL principles, educators need a robust assessment framework. Regular evaluations help teachers understand their application of UDL strategies and identify areas for improvement.

Assessment Tools

Checklists and Reflection Prompts: These tools enable ongoing self-assessment, helping educators reflect on their teaching practices and pinpoint areas for enhancement.
Student Feedback: Gathering feedback from students provides valuable insights into the effectiveness of UDL approaches. Encouraging students to share their experiences fosters a student-centered approach and ensures teaching methods align with learners' needs.

Planning for Future Improvements

- **Setting Specific Goals:** Establishing clear, measurable objectives can guide educators in their UDL journey. For example, a goal might be to integrate more interactive visual aids to cater to visual learners.
- **Collaboration with Colleagues:** Collaborating with peers fosters a supportive environment where educators can share experiences, resources, and ideas. This shared commitment to UDL principles can lead to innovative solutions and enhanced effectiveness.

Building a supportive community of practice

Creating a supportive network for educators through collaborative efforts is crucial for the successful implementation of UDL strategies. A community of practice fosters dialogue, mentorship, and resource sharing, enhancing teachers' ability to create inclusive classrooms.

Forming Professional Learning Communities (PLCs)

Professional Learning Communities (PLCs) serve as hubs where educators can regularly gather to discuss and refine their UDL practices. These structured meetings provide a platform for sharing insights, challenges, and successes, promoting continuous professional development.

- **Structured Meetings:** Facilitate resource and strategy sharing, allowing educators to brainstorm solutions to common classroom issues collaboratively.
- **Peer Observations:** Encouraging teachers to observe each other's classrooms fosters a culture of open feedback and mutual support, broadening perspectives and sparking innovative ideas.

Establishing Mentorship Opportunities

Mentorship programs pair experienced educators with those new to UDL, providing ongoing support and accountability. This relationship accelerates the learning curve and deepens the understanding of UDL principles.

- **Mentorship Benefits:** Mentors can guide mentees through the challenges of UDL implementation, offer advice based on experience, and provide emotional support.
- **Highlighting Positive Relationships:** Celebrating successful mentor-mentee relationships can serve as a model

for others, encouraging broader participation in mentorship programs.

Leveraging Technology for Collaboration

Digital tools enable educators to connect, share resources, and collaborate more effectively, regardless of location. Technology also supports remote and hybrid teaching models, enhancing accessibility and inclusivity.

- **Platforms for Collaboration:** Online forums, collaborative documents, and virtual meetings facilitate the exchange of ideas and materials among educators.
- **Virtual Professional Development:** Webinars, online courses, and virtual workshops expand access to training and expertise, allowing teachers to improve their skills without geographic constraints.

Celebrating Diversity in Teaching Strategies

Recognizing and valuing diverse teaching approaches fosters inclusivity within the educational community. Celebrating successes, regardless of size, creates a positive environment where educators feel valued and motivated to continue their efforts.

- **Highlighting Varied** Approaches: Sharing different methods for implementing UDL encourages innovative thinking and practices, leading to more effective teaching strategies.
- **Reinforcing Value of Contributions:** Emphasizing that all contributions are valuable builds a sense of ownership and commitment to the UDL process, encouraging educators to share freely and enrich the collective knowledge pool.

Teacher Self-Assessment Framework for UDL

A self-assessment framework helps educators reflect on their current practices and identify areas for growth in implementing UDL strategies. The framework is structured around the three core principles of UDL: Multiple Means of Engagement, Multiple Means of Representation, and Multiple Means of Action and Expression. It also includes a section on overall UDL implementation to assess a broader approach to inclusive teaching.

Self-Assessment Process:
A self-assessment framework helps educators reflect on their current practices and identify areas for growth in implementing UDL strategies.

The framework is structured around the three core principles of UDL:

- Multiple Means of Engagement
- Multiple Means of Representation
- Multiple Means of Action and Expression

It also includes a section on overall UDL implementation to help you assess your broader approach to inclusive teaching.

By using this self-assessment tool, you will:
- Gain insight into your current level of UDL implementation
- Identify specific areas where you excel in applying UDL principles
- Recognize opportunities for improvement in your teaching practices
- Set concrete goals for enhancing your use of UDL strategies
- Track your progress over time as you develop your UDL skills

Remember, this is not a test but a reflective tool for your professional growth.

To use the framework:

- Rate yourself on each item using the provided 1-5 scale
- Reflect on your ratings in each section
- Identify your strengths and areas for improvement
- Develop an action plan for enhancing your UDL implementation

We encourage you to revisit this self-assessment periodically (e.g., once per semester or school year) to track your progress and set new goals. You may also find it valuable to discuss your reflections with colleagues or instructional coaches to gain additional insights and support.

By committing to improving your UDL practices, you're taking an important step towards creating a more inclusive, effective learning environment for all your students. Let's begin the self-assessment and embark on this journey of professional growth together!

Rate your current level of implementation for each item on a scale of 1-5:
1 = Not Implemented
2 = Beginning implementation
3 = Partial implementation
4 = Substantial implementation
5 = Full implementation
☐

Self-assessment framework

Multiple Means of Engagement

I provide options for individual choice and autonomy in learning activities. [Rating]

I minimize threats and distractions in the learning environment. [Rating]

I vary the levels of challenge and support to optimize student engagement. [Rating]

I foster collaboration and community among students. [Rating]

I provide opportunities for students to self-reflect on their learning. [Rating]

Multiple Means of Representation

I offer information in multiple formats (e.g., text, audio, video, hands-on). [Rating]

I clarify vocabulary, symbols, and syntax for students. [Rating]

I provide options for students to customize the display of information. [Rating]

I highlight patterns, critical features, big ideas, and relationships in the content. [Rating]

I guide information processing, visualization, and manipulation. [Rating]

Multiple Means of Action and Expression

I provide multiple media for students to express their knowledge. [Rating]

I offer varied tools for composition and problem-solving. [Rating]

I support planning and strategy development for complex tasks. [Rating]

I provide scaffolds that can be gradually released with increasing independence. [Rating]

I offer opportunities for students to demonstrate their learning in multiple ways. [Rating]

Overall UDL Implementation

I design lessons with clear goals that allow for multiple means of achievement. [Rating]

I regularly assess and adjust my teaching methods based on UDL principles. [Rating]

I collaborate with colleagues to implement and improve UDL strategies. [Rating]

I communicate the benefits of UDL to students and parents. [Rating]

I continually seek professional development opportunities related to UDL. [Rating]

Reflection

Areas of Strength: [Write your reflections]

Areas for Improvement: [Write your reflections]

Next Steps for UDL Implementation: [Write your action plan]

Integrating UDL strategies into teaching practices requires a commitment to reflection, collaboration, and continuous improvement. By sharing successes, addressing challenges, building supportive communities, and utilizing self-assessment tools, educators can effectively implement UDL principles, fostering a more inclusive, engaging, and effective educational environment.

Conclusions

As we reach the end of our journey, it's important to reflect on the transformative power of Universal Design for Learning and how its core principles can enrich the educational experience. We have explored the three pillars of UDL: engagement, representation, and action & expression, understanding how each contributes to creating a more inclusive and equitable learning environment.

Engagement teaches us to capture students' interests and motivate them to participate actively. Representation reminds us of the importance of presenting information in diverse ways to reach all learning styles. Finally, action & expression encourage a variety of ways for students to demonstrate what they know, allowing each to express themselves according to their abilities and preferences. Together, these three principles work to ensure that every student has the opportunity to learn in a way that respects their uniqueness.

Bringing these principles into daily practice requires a consistent commitment and a willingness to embrace change. Think about how you might reorganize your classroom to promote flexible learning spaces or how you could introduce new technologies to offer alternative ways to acquire information and demonstrate understanding. Every small change can lead to significant improvements in how students engage with the material and with each other.

It's important to recognize that implementing UDL is a journey filled with both successes and challenges. Some strategies will work better than others, and that's perfectly fine. Reflecting on these experiences allows you to refine your approach and continuously improve. Sharing these reflections with colleagues can be a valuable opportunity to learn from one another and build a strong, supportive community of practice.

Imagine the lasting impact that UDL can have on your students: the shy student who finally finds a comfortable way to participate or the struggling learner who understands a concept through a new representation. These changes, even if small, can create a more inclusive and engaging learning environment.

Don't be afraid to start with small steps and build upon them over time. Every effort you make to integrate UDL principles into your teaching practice is a step forward towards a more equitable education system. Keep exploring, growing, and learning. Your dedication to this process will undoubtedly lead to positive outcomes for both your students and your professional growth.

Remember, UDL is not just a set of guidelines but a continuous journey of growth and adaptation. Embrace this journey with an open mind and a willingness to evolve, and you will make a significant impact on your students' learning experiences and the broader educational landscape.

Bibliography and Webliography

CAST (2018). Universal Design for Learning Guidelines version 2.2. Wakefield, MA: Author.

Meyer, A., Rose, D.H., & Gordon, D. (2014). Universal design for learning: Theory and practice. Wakefield, MA: CAST Professional Publishing.

Novak, K., & Rodriguez, K. (2016). Universally designed leadership: Applying UDL to systems and schools. Wakefield, MA: CAST Professional Publishing.

Ianes, D., & Cramerotti, S. (2013). Alunni con BES - Bisogni Educativi Speciali [Students with SEN - Special Educational Needs]. Trento: Erickson.

Canevaro, A. (2007). L'integrazione scolastica degli alunni con disabilità: Trent'anni di inclusione nella scuola italiana [School integration of students with disabilities: Thirty years of inclusion in Italian schools]. Trento: Erickson.

Hall, T.E., Meyer, A., & Rose, D.H. (Eds.). (2012). Universal design for learning in the classroom: Practical applications. New York: Guilford Press.

Cottini, L. (2017). Didattica speciale e inclusione scolastica [Special didactics and school inclusion]. Roma: Carocci editore.

Dalton, E.M., Mckenzie, J.A., & Kahonde, C. (2012). The implementation of inclusive education in South Africa: Reflections arising from a workshop for teachers and therapists to introduce Universal Design for Learning. African Journal of Disability, 1(1), 1-7.

Rao, K., Ok, M.W., & Bryant, B.R. (2014). A review of research on universal design educational models. Remedial and Special Education, 35(3), 153-166.

Pavone, M. (2014). L'inclusione educativa. Indicazioni pedagogiche per la disabilità [Educational inclusion. Pedagogical indications for disability]. Milano: Mondadori Università.

Basham, J.D., & Marino, M.T. (2013). Understanding STEM education and supporting students through universal design for learning. Teaching Exceptional Children, 45(4), 8-15.

Rose, D.H., & Meyer, A. (2002). Teaching every student in the digital age: Universal design for learning. Alexandria, VA: Association for Supervision and Curriculum Development.

D'Alessio, S. (2011). Inclusive education in Italy: A critical analysis of the policy of inclusive education. Rotterdam: Sense Publishers.

Booth, T., & Ainscow, M. (2016). Index for Inclusion: Developing learning and participation in schools. (Italian edition edited by F. Dovigo). Roma: Carocci editore.

Florian, L., & Black-Hawkins, K. (2011). Exploring inclusive pedagogy. British Educational Research Journal, 37(5), 813-828.
Slee, R. (2018). Inclusive education isn't dead; it just smells funny. London: Routledge.

Hehir, T., & Katzman, L. (2012). Effective inclusive schools: Designing successful schoolwide programs. John Wiley & Sons.

Mitchell, D. (2014). What really works in special and inclusive education: Using evidence-based teaching strategies. Routledge.

Tomlinson, C.A. (2014). The differentiated classroom: Responding to the needs of all learners. ASCD.

Ainscow, M., & Sandill, A. (2010). Developing inclusive education systems: the role of organisational cultures and leadership. International Journal of Inclusive Education, 14(4), 401-416.

Opertti, R., Walker, Z., & Zhang, Y. (2014). Inclusive education: From targeting groups and schools to achieving quality education as the core of EFA. In L. Florian (Ed.), The SAGE Handbook of Special Education: Two Volume Set (pp. 149-169). London: SAGE.

Caldin, R. (2013). Current pedagogic issues in inclusive education for the disabled. Pedagogia Oggi, 1(1), 11-25.

Dovigo, F. (2017). Pedagogia e didattica per realizzare l'inclusione: Guida all'Index [Pedagogy and didactics to achieve inclusion: Guide to the Index]. Roma: Carocci editore.

Wehmeyer, M.L. (2019). Strengths-based approaches to educating all learners with disabilities: Beyond special education. Teachers College Press.

Norwich, B. (2013). Addressing tensions and dilemmas in inclusive education: Living with uncertainty. Routledge.

CAST (Center for Applied Special Technology):
https://www.cast.org/

National Center on Universal Design for Learning:
http://www.udlcenter.org/

U.S. Department of Education - Office of Special Education Programs:
https://www2.ed.gov/about/offices/list/osers/osep/index.html

European Agency for Special Needs and Inclusive Education:
https://www.european-agency.org/

UNESCO - Inclusive Education:
https://en.unesco.org/themes/inclusion-in-education

National Disability Authority (Ireland) - Centre for Excellence in Universal Design:
http://universaldesign.ie/

Australian Government Department of Education - Disability Standards for Education:
https://www.education.gov.au/disability-standards-education-2005

Canadian Research Centre on Inclusive Education:
https://www.inclusiveeducationresearch.ca/

World Bank - Inclusive Education:
https://www.worldbank.org/en/topic/disability/brief/inclusive-education

United Nations - Convention on the Rights of Persons with Disabilities:
https://www.un.org/development/desa/disabilities/convention-on-the-rights-of-persons-with-disabilities.html

ABOUT THE AUTHOR

Roberto Russo's professional trajectory in education is deeply rooted in a unique blend of expertise in architecture and special education, which he leverages to develop innovative and inclusive teaching methodologies. After obtaining a Master's degree in Architecture in Italy, Roberto specialized in Special Education, merging these distinct disciplines to form a holistic approach to pedagogy that emphasizes accessibility and creativity.
He currently serves as an Art educator at the middle school level.

Outside the educational sphere, Roberto is actively engaged in the arts and cultural sectors, particularly within startup incubators and coworking spaces. This involvement is centered around the project "TeachFizz" which he developed to foster innovation in educational practices. Through "TeachFizz" Roberto collaborates with creative communities to stay at the forefront of emerging trends.

Publications:
- **"UDL in Action**: Over 60 Universal Design for Learning Lesson Plans and Tools for Teachers in K-12 Classrooms " (2024)
- **"Engage Students with UDL**: A Practical Guide to Universal Design for Learning with Guideline, Strategies and Lesson Plans for Teacher" (2024)

Made in the USA
Las Vegas, NV
25 November 2024

12656114R00101